Physical Characteristics of the Shih Tzu

(from the American Kennel Club's breed standard)

Body: Short-coupled and sturdy with no waist or tuck-up. The Shih Tzu is slightly longer than tall.

Tail: Set on high, heavily plumed, carried in curve well over back.

Coat: Luxurious, double-coated, dense, long, and flowing. Slight wave permissible. Hair on top of head Is tied up.

Size: Ideally, height at withers is 9 to 10.5 inches; but, not less than 8 inches nor more than 11 inches. Ideally, weight of mature dogs, 9 to 16 pounds.

Feet: Firm, well-padded, point straight ahead.

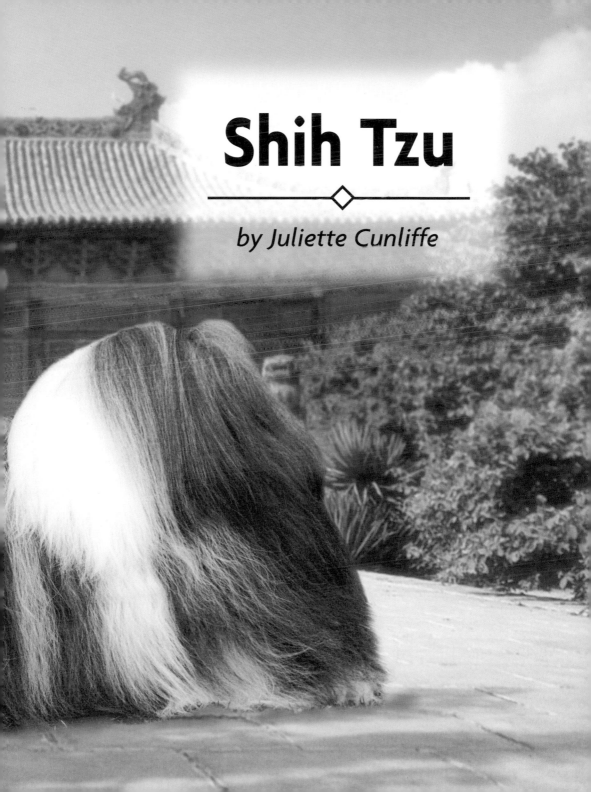

Shih Tzu

by Juliette Cunliffe

9

History of the Shih Tzu

Examine the Shih Tzu's history as the author reveals the breed's beginnings in ancient Tibet and China; follow its evolution from the highly esteemed pet of Asian emperors to its establishment in the US and beyond.

22

Characteristics of the Shih Tzu

Discover what makes the Shih Tzu such a unique and impressive dog: his practical size, glorious coat and confident personality all qualify the Shih Tzu as a charming and hardy pet for the right owner or family. Also learn about breed-specific health concerns common in some Shih Tzu.

33

Breed Standard for the Shih Tzu

Learn the requirements of a well-bred Shih Tzu by studying the description of the breed set forth in the American Kennel Club standard. Both show dogs and pets must possess key characteristics as outlined in the breed standard.

38

Your Puppy Shih Tzu

Know how to choose a reputable breeder and a healthy, typical Shih Tzu puppy. Understand the responsibilities of ownership, including home preparation, acclimatization, visiting the vet and prevention of common puppy problems.

64

Everyday Care of Your Shih Tzu

Enter into a sensible discussion of dietary and feeding considerations, exercise, grooming, traveling and identification of your dog. This chapter discusses Shih Tzu care for all stages of development.

84

Training Your Shih Tzu

By Charlotte Schwartz
Be informed about the importance of training your Shih Tzu from the basics of house-training and understanding the development of a young dog to executing basic obedience commands (sit, stay, down, etc.).

Contents

Health Care of Your Shih Tzu   **109**

Discover how to select a qualified veterinarian and care for your dog at all stages of life. Topics include vaccination scheduling, skin problems, dealing with external and internal parasites and common medical conditions.

Your Senior Shih Tzu   **135**

Recognize the signs of an aging dog, both behavioral and medical; implement a senior-care program with your veterinarian and become comfortable with making the final decisions and arrangements for your senior Shih Tzu.

Showing Your Shih Tzu   **142**

Experience the dog show world, including different types of shows and the making of an American Kennel Club champion. Go beyond the conformation ring to obedience and agility trials, etc.

Index 156

KENNEL CLUB BOOKS® SHIH TZU
ISBN 13: 978-1-59378-216-0

Copyright © 2003 • Kennel Club Books® • A Division of BowTie, Inc.
40 Broad Street, Freehold, New Jersey 07728 USA
Cover Design Patented: US 6,435,559 B2 • Printed in South Korea

Photography by Carol Ann Johnson,
with additional photographs by:

Norvia Behling, Carolina Biological Supply, Doskocil, Isabelle Francais, James Hayden-Yoav, James R. Hayden, RBP, Bill Jonas, Dwight R. Kuhn, Dr. Dennis Kunkel, Mikki Pet Products, Phototake, Jean Claude Revy, Alice Roche, Dr. Andrew Spielman, Karen Taylor, and C. James Webb

Illustrations by Patricia Peters and Renée Low.

The publisher wishes to thank Madame Annie Bondier, Tina Marie Izzo, Tom and Sheila Richardson, Maria and Richard Smolen, Les and Betty Williams and P. Michael Shea-Zackin and the rest of the owners of Shih Tzu featured in this book.

This ancient ink and color drawing on silk
appears in a scroll executed by Chou Fang from
the T'ang Dynasty (618–907 A.D.). The scroll
depicts ladies in waiting, teasing a Shih Tzu with
their insect-chasing whip.

HISTORY OF THE
Shih Tzu

The Shih Tzu is an Asian breed whose ancestry lies both in Tibet and in China. As a result, some of today's enthusiasts consider it a Tibetan breed while others more closely associate this adorable little dog with China.

TIBETAN BACKGROUND
Although there have been times when the Chinese and Tibetans have cooperated with each other, since the seventh century there has frequently been strife between the two nations. For the sake of diplomacy, Tibetan nobles sometimes took Chinese brides of royal rank. It therefore follows that gifts were exchanged between people of these two great cultures in which mythology abounds. Often these gifts were

The history of the Shih Tzu, meaning *lion mane* in Chinese, was closely intermingled with the Tibetan Chinese politics during the T'ang Dynasty.

dogs. The Lhasa Apso, a Tibetan breed and direct ancestor of the Shih Tzu, is said to have existed since 800 B.C., but there is no tangible evidence of this as written historical records in Tibet were not kept until around A.D. 639.

Because the Shih Tzu descended from the Tibetan Lhasa Apso, Tibet is considered the earliest ancestral home of the Shih Tzu. Dogs were given as tribute gifts for safe passage from Tibet to China, the long journey by caravan taking eight to ten

ANCESTRY: CHINA
Over the years, various theories have been put forward regarding the origin of the Shih Tzu. According to one theory, three temple dogs were sent to China around 1650, and from these dogs came the Shih Tzu.

9

The Cheltenham Show of 1933, the year before the Tibetan breed standards were sorted out! Here are prominent British fanciers, from left to right: Lady Brownrigg with Hibou, Yangtse and Shu-ssa; Miss Hutchins with Lung-fu-ssu and Tang; General Sir Douglas Brownrigg with Hzu-Hsi and Miss Marjorie Wild with one of her Lhasa Apsos.

months. The Tibetan Lhasa Apsos were not considered sacred animals, but they were treated as prized possessions nonetheless. They were only given as gifts never sold. The dogs were undoubtedly held in high esteem, for it was believed that they carried the souls of monks who had erred in their previous lives.

Buddhism spread from India into Tibet in the seventh century but was not adopted in China until 1253, at the time of Kublai Khan. The lion, in various mythological forms, plays an important part in Buddhism. Indeed the

ANCESTRY: IRELAND

The Shih Tzu first arrived in Ireland with Miss Hutchins in 1928 but, until the Second World War, the breed was only known in Variety classes there. In the mid-1960s the breed grew numerically stronger, and Shih Tzu in Ireland are now fairly popular. The Irish breeders strive hard and are truly dedicated to the breed.

The Tibetans would refer to Shih Tzu as "Apsok," a name used to refer to all long-coated dogs.

Buddha Manjusri, who is the god of learning, is believed to travel around as a simple priest with a small dog. This dog, called a Ha-pa, can instantly be transformed into a lion so that the Buddha can ride on its back. The snow lion, though, is considered the king of animals and it is with this white mythological beast that the Shih Tzu and Lhasa Apso are most closely connected. The snow lion is believed to be so powerful that when it roars, seven dragons fall out of the sky.

Tibetans have always drawn distinction between the "true" lion and the "dog" lion, but have never been too clear about the naming of their breeds. Without doubt, some crossing took place between the various Tibetan breeds. Even today it is possible to breed together two fully-coated Lhasa Apsos or Shih Tzu and produce one or more puppies that look like pure-bred Tibetan Spaniels. This may come as something of a shock, but is clearly a throwback to earlier days. Interestingly, the Tibetans refer to all long-coated dogs as

ANCESTRY: SWITZERLAND
Although it cannot be confirmed that there were no Shih Tzu in the country before the 1950s, the first Shih Tzu registration in Switzerland was in 1956. This was the bitch Di Ji Anjou, who was imported from the Countess d'Anjou in France.

"Apsok," which further complicates the issue when trying to research the history of Tibetan breeds.

We know that the Shih Tzu can be traced back to dogs of Tibetan origin. We must also look at the dogs that were in China at that time, as these are the dogs with which the early Shih Tzu ancestors were crossed.

CHINESE BACKGROUND

The "square dogs" that were accepted by a Chinese emperor in 1760 B.C. are believed to have been of Chow Chow type, although we do not know their size. However, in 500 B.C., there are known to have been not only dogs that followed their masters' chariots but also others with short mouths. These latter dogs were carried in the carts, so we can safely assume that they were

ANCESTRY: GREAT BRITAIN

In Britain, progeny from the Pekingese/Shih Tzu cross of the 1950s could not be registered as pure-bred Shih Tzu until the third filial generation. However, in the United States, a further three generations were required prior to registration.

fairly small. It has been said that the nasal bones of puppies in China were broken with chopsticks to shorten them, although the skull of an early short-nosed dog housed in the British Museum has a naturally short nose, the bones unbroken.

By the end of the first century A.D., emperors clearly took an interest in small dogs. A short-legged dog, known as the "Pai" dog, belonged under the table. This may not appear especially significant until one considers that, since the people sat on the floor to eat, Chinese tables were very low. These dogs must therefore have been very small indeed. Great honors were bestowed on these small dogs; in fact, in A.D. 168, one was even awarded the highest literary rank of the period. Many male dogs were given the rank of K'ai Fu, which is just below the rank of Viceroy, while bitches were given ranks of the wives of such officials. These fortunate dogs had soldiers to guard them and carpets to sleep on, and they were fed only on the choicest meat.

By A.D. 1300, "golden-coated nimble dogs" were commonly bred by people in their homes. These dogs were described as resembling the lion; indeed the Emperor of that time apparently used to love them so much that he stole them from his subjects. In China there were various small breeds of dog, including the Pug, but by 1820 the cult of the lap dog reigned supreme. Very tiny dogs, known as "sleeve dogs," were the height of fashion. As their name implies, they were kept in voluminous Chinese sleeves. It is still believed that their growth was stunted by artificial means; food supply was restricted and puppies were kept in wire cages until they reached maturity. Thankfully the

A modern Lhasa Apso. Though distinctive from the Shih Tzu, the relationship between the two breeds is evident.

Dowager Empress Tzu Hsi, a great lover of dogs, objected to artificial dwarfing and soon these tiny dogs fell out of fashion, finding themselves referred to instead as "lump-headed dogs."

THE DOWAGER EMPRESS TZU HSI

The Dowager Empress kept over a hundred Pekingese and laid down many palace rules for her dogs. Among these was the stipulation that they must be "dainty in their food," so that by their fastidiousness they might be known as Imperial Dogs. Their diets consisted of such delicacies as sharks' fins and curlews' livers, antelope milk, the juice of custard apple, rhinoceros horn and the clarified fat of sacred leopard. In an effort to stub their noses, the Empress stroked and massaged the olfactory organs of her dogs, and they chewed on leather tightly stretched on a frame.

In 1908 His Holiness the Dalai Lama presented the Dowager Empress with several dogs. These were described as similar to the breed of lion dog then seen in Peking. She called these her "Shih Tzu Kou," and kept them apart from her Pekingese to maintain the breed characteristics of these treasured gifts. However, these "Shih Tzu Kou" did not arrive long before the death of the Empress. Although the palace eunuchs continued to breed them, it is highly likely that experimen-

tal crosses took place, thus creating a divergence in type. It is generally believed that the eunuchs bred three types of shortnosed dogs: the Pug, the Pekingese and another long-haired dog known as the Shih Tzu.

THE SHIH TZU LEAVES CHINA
Lady Brownrigg and her husband, who was later to become General Sir Douglas Brownrigg, acquired their first Shih Tzu in 1928. They had heard of "Tibetan Lion Dogs" or "Shock-dogs" owned by Chinese emperors, and understood that the best were to be found in Peking, where they were then living. They had seen a small black-and-white dog that rather took their fancy, and were determined to get one

The Pekingese was the favorite of the Dowager Empress Tzu Hsi. In 1908, she was presented with lion dogs as a gift from the Dalai Lama. These were not interbred with the Pekingese of the Empress.

that was similar. The first bitch they acquired was already in whelp but, sadly, she died. However, with the help of Mme. Wellington Koo, they soon found another black-and-white bitch, born in 1927. Named "Shu-ssa," she had a white "apple mark" on her head and a black patch on her tail and side. The Brownriggs thought she looked like a fluffy baby owl, with her expressive eyes and hair sticking out all around her face. Her coat was thick and her tail curled over her back.

Dogs such as Shu-ssa were not often seen in public places, for they were usually kept in homes and courtyards. It was also understood that the palace eunuchs had some of these dogs, and that others had been bred by French and Russian people living in China. A Frenchman, Dr. Cenier owned a black-and-white dog of this kind, and the dog, "Hibou," came into the possession of the Brownriggs.

Also in China at that time was Miss E. M. Hutchins and she, too, had acquired a dog. The dog was called Lung-fu-ssu, born in 1926. Also black-and-white, Lung-fu-ssu was heavier and coarser than those of the Brownriggs; he had a wavy coat and his tail was carried rather loosely.

In 1930 Miss Hutchins returned to England, bringing with her four dogs: the Brownriggs' Shu-ssa and Hibou, Lung-fu-ssu

The Shih Tzu's worldwide popularity knows no bounds! The inspiration for artists for centuries, the breed has been preserved in every medium imaginable. Here a Scandinavian artist displays her work at a club show.

and a bitch called Mei Mei. Mei Mei was tragically killed by a Sealyham after coming out of quarantine. The three surviving dogs weighed between 12 lbs 1 oz and 14 lbs 9 oz. Although Lady Brownrigg was aware that there were other smaller dogs in China, these were not used for breeding.

THE BREED IN BRITAIN
Shu-ssa was mated to Hibou and produced a litter in quarantine in

> **TINIES ON THE RISE**
> Subsequent to the introduction of the Pekingese cross in Shih Tzu breeding programs, in 1956 a private club was set up to promote the smaller size of Shih Tzu, known as "tinies." Initially the British Kennel Club refused permission, but permission later was granted when the club's aims had been altered.

April 1930. England, of course, has had strict quarantine laws for many years, though less so presently. At that time, it was possible for puppies born in quarantine to be released after eight

The Chow Chow breed is believed to be the square Chinese dog favored by the emperor. Like the Shih Tzu, the Chow Chow is groomed in homage to the lion.

weeks, so the puppies were carefully homed. Shu-ssa had two other litters, one later that same year, sired by Lung-fu-ssu, and another in 1932, sired again by Hibou.

By now there were several types of long-coated foreign dog in Britain. Colonel and Mrs. Bailey had brought back Apsos to Britain in 1928, Colonel Bailey having taken over from Sir Charles Bell as Political Officer for Tibet in 1921. This was the

beginning of a traumatic time to follow.

A club called "The Apso and Lion Dog Club" was formed, and the first show to be held for the "breed" was the West of England Kennel Club Show in 1933. At this show, it became immediately apparent that the dogs being exhibited differed greatly, especially in length of foreface. The judge was Colonel Bailey, who made no secret of the fact that he thought the dogs imported from China were different. He expressed the belief that they had been crossed with Pekingese. What became known as "the battle of the noses" had begun!

Much heated debate and correspondence took place between the parties involved, and with The Kennel Club. It was suggested that the two types were differentiated by the names "Apsos, Chinese Type" and "Apsos, Tibetan Type," but this did not reach fruition. Instead they agreed to The Kennel Club's suggestion of separating the dogs that had heralded from China from the Tibetan dogs. The Chinese dogs were to be re-registered as Shih Tzu.

Understandably, it was becoming impossible to judge the two breeds in the same classes at shows, but this had to be done until the separation had officially taken place. The debate continued and there was much confusion over breed names, for many owners of the dogs we now know as Shih Tzu wished to keep the word "Tibetan" in the breed's name. They continued to refer to their breed as "Tibetan Lion Dogs," which did not go over well with the Apso followers. In 1934 the Tibetan Breeds Association was formed, but the Shih Tzu fraternity was not included. There was much press coverage about the heated debate concerning the two breeds, but as was said in *Our Dogs'* "Foreign Dog Fancies" of June 22, 1934, "...while the Apso and Shih Tzu devotees are both standing by their guns, there is no ill-feeling on either side."

THE SECOND WORLD WAR

The problem of the difference between the breeds we now know as the Lhasa Apso and the Shih Tzu was solved, and by 1939 the number of Shih Tzu registered with The Kennel Club was 183. In 1940, instead of being registered under "Any Other Variety," the Shih Tzu was granted a separate register and became eligible for Challenge Certificates, the "tickets" needed to earn a championship in the UK. However, the next major problem to occur was the Second World War, so Challenge Certificates had to wait.

Lady Brownrigg was heavily involved with work for the Red Cross. The groomings from her dogs' coats were spun into yarn,

which was used to knit articles to aid the Red Cross. Breeding virtually ceased and it was a struggle to preserve the breed, which was only one of many in danger of dying out.

Following the war, a few of the original breeders resumed their showing and breeding activities. There had been a few more imports and, in an endeavor to preserve the breed, all dogs (often regardless of their quality) were used for breeding. This is the reason that some of the dogs seen at that time were far removed from the breed we know today.

THE FIRST UK CHAMPION

One of the only two Shih Tzu registered with The Kennel Club during 1945 was Ta Chi of Taishan, who was to become the breed's very first champion. She descended from a Norwegian import, Choo-Choo, owned by Queen Elizabeth I. Ta Chi of Taishan's sire was Sui-Yan and her dam was Madam Ko of

Through hundreds of years of selective breeding, the Shih Tzu still maintains those physical and mental characteristics that the Chinese and Tibetans found so desirable.

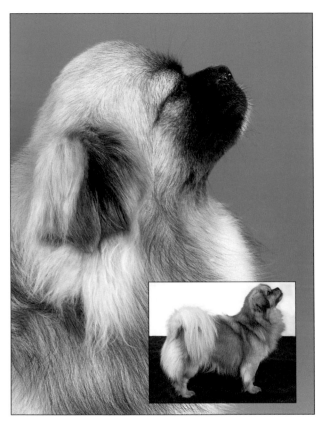

A Tibetan cousin that is closer than you think! Clip away the Shih Tzu's coat and his resemblance to the Tibetan Spaniel is enlightening! As evident in the close-up, the Tibetan Spaniel's head is smaller and less round than that of the Shih Tzu.

Taishan. The first champion was very highly regarded and even today there are those who still feel she was one of the most typical specimens of the breed.

THE SHIH TZU IN AMERICA

In 1936 the American Kennel Club (AKC) had received an application to register a Shih Tzu, and they made the erroneous statement that "the Lhassa Terrier and Shih Tzu are one and the same breed." Britain's Tibetan Breeds Association became

involved, explaining the differences between the two.

Despite several articles appearing in the American press concerning the two different breeds, Shih Tzu from the UK were exported to the US but incorrectly registered in the US as Lhasa Apsos. This was not corrected until 1950, and during the years in between many were bred from. This problem, as will be appreciated, affected the Lhasa Apso far more than it did the Shih Tzu, resulting in Shih Tzu blood flowing in the veins of many Lhasa Apsos, even today. However, these early problems also had a negative effect on the Shih Tzu for they undoubtedly delayed its recognition in America as a separate breed.

The Pekingese-Shih Tzu cross also had an important bearing on the breed in America. In Britain the progeny of the third filial generation cross were registered as Shih Tzu, but in the US a further three generations had to be bred from the original cross before pure-bred registrations were accepted. So it was that it took until 1955 before the breed received official status in America, because only then were enthusiastic breeders able to offer sufficient proof that there was nationwide interest in the Shih Tzu. It was initially accepted as 1 of 13 breeds that could be exhibited in the Miscellaneous Class and the first recorded public appearance of the Shih Tzu was at the Philadelphia Show in 1957.

By 1960 the Texas Shih Tzu Society and the Shih Tzu Club of America had been formed, and a gentleman by the name of Mr. Curtis was also actively involved in registering his own Shih Tzu with the AKC. The two clubs eventually combined, but Mr. Curtis did not participate in that merger. So in 1963 the American Shih Tzu Club was formed and a Stud Book was maintained. In July of that year, 369 Shih Tzu of American and foreign breeding were recorded.

In 1964 the first match show for this breed took place. Held at the home of Ingrid Coleman in Pennsylvania, there were 51 Shih Tzu entered under judge Mrs. Eunice Clark of Ohio. Winning Best in Match was Margaret Easton's all black Si-Kiang Wu-Ling, bred by Mrs. Ingrid Colwell, whose Swedish import, Ch. Jungfeltets Jung Wu, took the award for Best of Opposite Sex. Both were descended from Scandinavian Ch. Bjornholm Wu-Ling.

A group of early dedicated breeders did much to promote the Shih Tzu, and by now it was becoming fashionable in America. A second match took place in 1965, this judged by Audrey Fowler of the UK. Things had progressed sufficiently that on March 16, 1969, the American Kennel Club allowed registration in its Stud Book, for by then there were around 3,000 Shih Tzu eligible for registration. A fascinating fact is that between the years 1960 and 1969 there were 642 imports from the UK.

Five months after the Stud Book was opened, the Shih Tzu had its very first opportunity to compete for championship points in America, and on that first day Rev. and Mrs. D. Allan Easton's three-year-old Canadian Ch. Chumulari Ying Ying took Best in Show (BIS) at the New Brunswick Kennel Club Show in New Jersey, under judge James Trullinger. The breed judge was Alva Rosenberg, and there had been 970 dogs entered at the show. On the same day elsewhere, two other Shih Tzu won their Toy Groups, Int. Ch. Bjornholmes Pif (sire of the BIS winner) and Lakoya Princess Tanya, a one-year-old granddaughter of Pif.

Bjornholmes Pif had been imported from Denmark the previous year and had already gained his championship title in five different countries. He went on to become the first Shih Tzu champion in the US, having amassed the necessary 15 championship points in only 13 days. The following year, he tied for the award of "Top Producing Toy Sire."

The first Shih Tzu bitch to

gain her title in the US was Ch. Chumulari Hih-Hih, a daughter of the BIS winner at the match in 1964, and another who gained her necessary points in 13 days. Ch. Lakoya Princess Tanya Shu soon followed with her title, and that year 93 Shih Tzu gained their titles. Over half of these were sired by just eight stud dogs. From then on, the Shih Tzu went on to gain rapid popularity, with the first specialty show with championship points held at Portland, Oregon in 1973.

PIONEERS IN AMERICA

We have already read about Rev. D. Allan Easton and his wife, Margaret, co-owners of the Chumulari affix. It was Rev. Easton who saw what were believed to have been the last two Shih Tzu to leave Peking. These were bred by Alfred Kohen and purchased by the British Consul. The first Shih Tzu the Eastons managed to buy was Si-Kiang's Tashi, in 1961. They also imported Wei-Honey Gold of Elfann and Jemima of Lhakang from England, and later Swiss and Czechoslovakian Ch. Tangra v. Tschomo Lungma, from Germany. This bitch, who went on to become a Canadian champion, was in whelp when she came to America and produced the famous Am-Can. Ch. Chumulari Ying Ying, who sired at least 29 champions.

Ingrid Colwell (Si-Kiang) was another of the breed's pioneers in America. She was born in Sweden, the daughter of a breeder, and purchased her first Shih Tzu in Germany in 1958. She came to the US in 1960, bringing with her four Shih Tzu that formed her foundation stock. This enthusiastic breeder was soon joined by the import Jungfaltets Wu-Pa. It was so very sad that Ingrid Colwell died tragically in 1968.

Mary and Jack Woods (Mariljac) obtained their first Shih Tzu from the UK in 1959 and were instrumental in helping to set up the American Shih Tzu Club. After the death of her husband, Mrs. Wood continued breeding under the same affix with Norman Patton of Dragonwyck fame. Among his many top-winning Shih Tzu is Ch. Dragonwyck The Great Gatsby.

Bill and Joan Kibler's Encore Chopsticks won the Shih Tzu Club's specialty for six consecutive years. Although he himself was retired by the time the breed was recognized in 1969, he certainly made his mark on the breed, for he sired no fewer than 14 champions.

Margaret Edel (Mar-Del) was also involved in the breed's early struggle for recognition. She acquired her first stock from Ingrid Colwell and bred one of the country's top producers, Ch. Mar-Del's Ring-A-Ding-Ding. Another who obtained his first Shih Tzu

These Austrian Shih Tzu were exhibited in Slovenia.

from Ingrid Colwell was Andy Hickok Warner (Rosemar), as did Pat Semones Durham (Pa-Sha and Si-Kiang).

As time moved on, more and more dedicated breeders and exhibitors joined the ranks of those mentioned, and the breed went from strength to strength so that it is now in the top ten most popular breeds in America. A truly remarkable story of a breed's success!

THE SHIH TZU IN EUROPE

In Scandinavia, Norway was the founder of Shih Tzu history, for the Danish Minister to China and his wife took the breed to Norway in 1932. The first Shih Tzu kennel in Denmark was set up in the 1940s, while the breed did not arrive in Sweden until 1950 and in Finland until 1955.

Mrs. Erika Geusendam's Kennel von Tschomo-Lungma was the first Shih Tzu kennel in Germany, founded in 1960. In the Netherlands, the leading kennel of the 1960s was that of Mrs. Eta Pauptit, who had made a careful study of British and Scandinavian kennels before founding her own.

Shih Tzu did not arrive in what are now the Czech and Slovak Republics until 1980, but in France the story was different. The Countess d'Anjou had bred Shih Tzu in Peking long before the Chinese Revolution and had introduced the breed to France in 1950. She was responsible for writing the first standard of the breed in her country. By the 1980s the breed had become very popular in France, and is now catered for by enthusiastic clubs dedicated to a small group of similar breeds.

21

CHARACTERISTICS OF THE
Shih Tzu

Apart from his incredible good looks, the Shih Tzu also has a most appealing character and is of manageable size. To keep a Shih Tzu in gloriously long coat does take a lot of work, so that is an important consideration, but a pet Shih Tzu can, of course, be kept in short coat if an owner prefers.

The Shih Tzu has become a highly popular breed, in recent years having been ranked in the top ten breeds in the US. With around 20,000 new AKC registrations each year, the Shih Tzu is numerically the strongest breed in the Toy Group.

Shih Tzu are among the most popular breeds in the US, ranking in the top ten breeds. Surely the face of a Shih Tzu pup explains the age-old fascination with the breed.

PHYSICAL CHARACTERISTICS

The Shih Tzu is a fairly small breed, though not as small as some of his fellow Toy breeds. Nonetheless, he is strong and sturdy for his size. The ideal height is not more than 10.5 inches and the ideal weight ranges between 10 to 16 lbs, although some Shih Tzu are a little heavier. Because of their sturdiness, Shih Tzu are perfectly capable of going for long walks, yet short walks suit them just fine as well; they are highly adaptable to either situation.

HEAD

The head of the Shih Tzu has to be one of his most appealing physical attributes. A "chrysanthemum-like face" undoubtedly helps to give the Shih Tzu his delightful expression. Apart from the fact that the hair on the head is tied up in a topknot, the head of the Shih Tzu is quite different

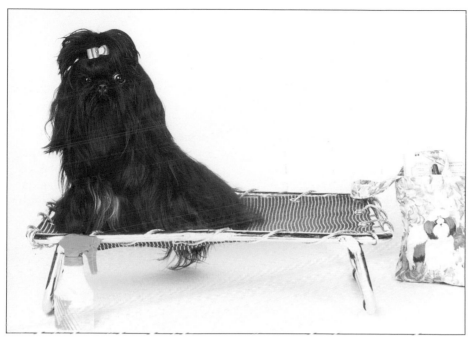

The Shih Tzu's glorious coat requires much dedication from an owner. Kept in full-length show coat, the Shih Tzu must be groomed daily.

than that of the Lhasa Apso and that of the Pekingese, falling as it does somewhere between the two. The Shih Tzu's foreface is not as long as that of the Apso, and the Shih Tzu's skull is broader, but compared to the Pekingese, the Shih Tzu's foreface is longer and the skull is not as flat. Due to the skull shape, the eye of the Shih Tzu should be fuller than that of the Apso.

COLORS AND COAT

A Shih Tzu in full show coat is a glorious sight, but to keep a coat in this condition certainly involves time and dedication. Not only does the Shih Tzu have a long, flowing top coat but it also has a substantial undercoat. This means that merely grooming the top layer may initially give a reasonably good overall appearance, but in no time at all the undercoat will start to form knots. Knots and tangles are incredibly

COLORFUL DESCRIPTIONS

The Chinese historically have had some fascinating ways of describing the various attributes of the Shih Tzu. The head has been variously described as "owl head," "lion head" and "water chestnut face," while the mouth has been called a "water caltrop mouth," "frog mouth" and "charcoal heater mouth."

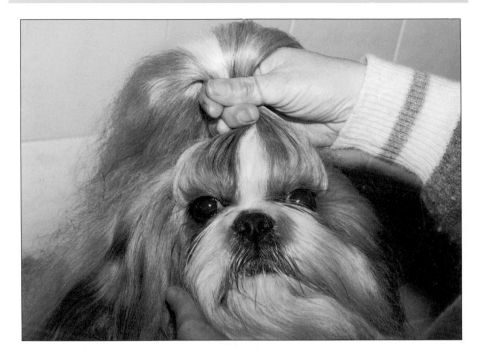

The art of tying the topknot. The breed's correct expression is dependent on properly tying up the headfall.

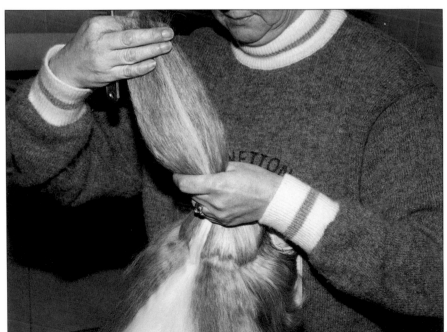

difficult to remove if allowed to build up, so this aspect of coat care must be taken seriously into consideration before setting your heart on the breed.

A topknot tied correctly can enhance the features of a dog, but an incorrectly groomed topknot can just as easily spoil the expression. Undoubtedly, doing up a Shih Tzu's headfall to best effect is an art that may take the novice months, and sometimes even years, of practice! In addition to a colorful bow tied at the center of the topknot, some groomers pad out the topknot with cotton to give it a more impressive look!

Many Shih Tzu pets are, however, kept in short coat, known usually as the "pet trim." Although this can be done at home, many owners find it easier to have the coat professionally trimmed about three times each year, although attention to the

Groomers top the Shih Tzu's head with a colorful bow.

coat is, of course, still necessary between trims.

The Shih Tzu can be found in a wide variety of colors, for all are permissible. Colors range through various shades of gold to red and grays through to black. Of course, there are also parti-colors, which are predominantly white with another color. In parti-colors, a white marking on the forehead and tail tip are highly prized. In Shih Tzu, you can even find dogs that are liver in color. These are actually permitted, although in this case the nose is liver in color, rather than black, to correspond with the coat.

Because there is no color preference in Shih Tzu, in truth

AN ARISTOCRAT

In 1935 Madam Lu Zuen Lee, an experienced breeder of Shih Tzu, considered the general behavior of the breed aristocratic, noting that even in the poorest quarters he was well cared for. This, she felt, indicated the fine strain from which these dogs had been bred, and that they imposed their qualities upon their surroundings.

The parti-colored Shih Tzu has white markings on the forehead and tail tip, and, of course, white must be the predominant coat color.

TAILS AND DEWCLAWS

The tail of the Shih Tzu should always be carried gaily, well over the back. As with the rest of the dog's coat, the tail coat will need regular attention for it, too, is long and flowing. However, because of the breed's compact size, the tail is unlikely to knock your precious knick-knacks to the floor, as might the enthusiastic tail of a larger dog such as a Dalmatian or Labrador Retriever. A Shih Tzu's tail can indeed be an enthusiastic one, but discreetly so. It is never docked.

Regarding dewclaws, many breeders do like to have them removed when puppies are three days old. This makes nails easier to manage under the long adult coat. Removing the dewclaws is permissible according to the breed standard.

PERSONALITY

The Shih Tzu is described as being intelligent, active, alert, friendly and independent. This is indeed an intelligent breed, though not one that demands to be constantly given new things to do as with many larger breeds. The Shih Tzu will use his own intelligence and ingenuity to find things to do, and to watch a Shih Tzu carefully planning out what little activity to play next can be highly amusing for the onlooker—provided that the new game selected is one that will not cause any damage!

an owner should not be swayed by color. Having said that, it is only natural that some people have a purely personal preference, just as they might for the color of their car or furniture. What really matters is the quality of the dog's construction, temperament and coat. However, if choosing a pet, color may indeed be a deciding factor, and this is entirely understandable. After all, there is no point in buying a black Shih Tzu and, love the dog as you might, thinking for the next 14 years or so that it was a pity you didn't find the golden color you really preferred!

Shih Tzu are undoubtedly alert to sounds and happenings around them, but they may or may not decide to take an active part in the goings-on—that is their personality. They will decide what they want to do and, although an endearingly friendly breed, they will make up their own minds about how much or how little they choose to be involved.

This is neither a snappy nor an excessively noisy breed, though a Shih Tzu, like other dogs, will usually enjoy a good bark when the fancy takes him. Shih Tzu love to be with people. They are never happier than when with their owners, so they prefer to live as part of a family than in a kennel situation. Although some Shih Tzu do take part in obedience and agility competitions, they are not renowned for being a particularly obedient breed because of their somewhat independent nature.

Most Shih Tzu get along extremely well with other dogs, and often owners find they can keep several dogs, both males and females, together. Of course individual temperaments vary, so you

That the Shih Tzu is a "people dog" goes without saying. These little fur persons thrive on interaction with their devoted and caring humans.

must always introduce dogs to each other under close supervision, especially males. Although by no means aggressive by nature, males will usually stand their ground when attacked. In some cases, it is therefore not a good idea to keep together males that have been used at stud, for one is sure to become the more dominant and the other dog may just not agree to that! Females can be rather more temperamental around the time of their seasons, so again caution should be exercised. In general, though, Shih Tzu are highly sociable animals in every sense of the word.

HEALTH CONSIDERATIONS

The Shih Tzu is a hardy little dog and usually a fairly healthy breed. A few suffer from veterinary and possibly hereditary problems, but this is not a breed with many major hereditary problems associated with it. There are a few common conditions, though, to which the potential owner should be alerted.

Although the majority of Shih Tzu have wide-open nostrils, tight nostrils do appear to be an inherited condition in this breed. Nostrils that are tight can be apparent at birth but sometimes cannot be noticed until between ten days and three weeks of age. However, when a puppy is old enough for sale, it should be clear whether the nostrils are affected or not.

At birth, nostrils can be so tight that they are effectively deformed and curve inwards. In other cases, the nostrils are sufficiently wide at birth but tighten soon after, probably because of varying growth rate in the puppy. The nostrils usually correct themselves with time, but urgent veterinary advice should be sought nonetheless. If left to his own devices and the problem does not correct itself, such a puppy will probably grow weak and die as a result. A teaspoon of brandy added to each cup of feed has been found to help, as has keeping the puppy's environment at a constant temperature.

A condition that does not usually present a real problem, but that can frighten a new owner, is known as "the puffs." This is a fairly frequent occurrence in brachycephalic (short-nosed) breeds. Because of elongation of the soft palate, a dog suddenly draws in short, sharp breaths and looks very tense, usually standing four square as he does so. This is usually brought on by the dog's becoming very excited, but usually only lasts a matter of seconds. A quick and simple solution is to place your fingers over the dog's nostrils, thereby causing

THE HAIR OF THE DOG

Chinese depictions of the coat colors found in the Shih Tzu are highly descriptive and illustrative. A completely black dog was called "Yi Ting Mo," or "lump of ink," while one with black body and white feet was known as "Hsueh Li Chan," translated as "standing in snow." A dog with a yellow coat and white neck was called "Chin Pi Yu Huang," meaning "golden cape with a white collar," and the term "Pien Ta Shiu Chiu," or "whipping the embroidered balls," described the coat pattern of a dog with round yellow patches.

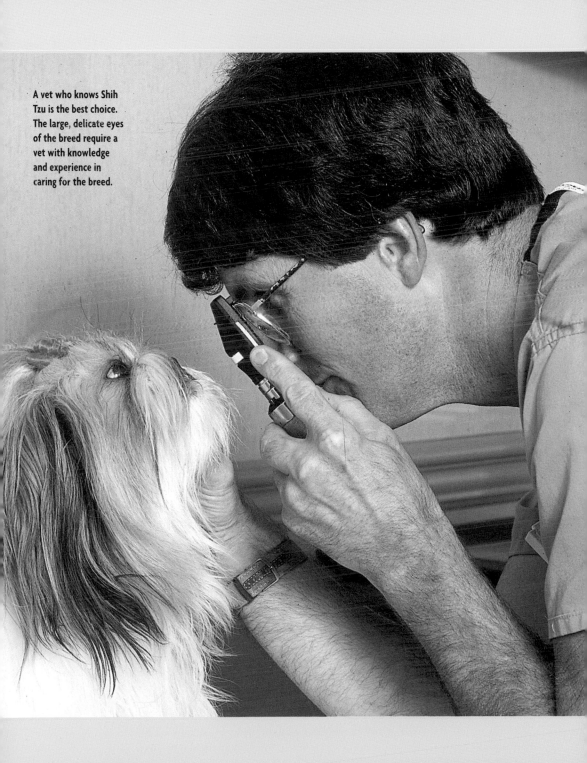

A vet who knows Shih Tzu is the best choice. The large, delicate eyes of the breed require a vet with knowledge and experience in caring for the breed.

him to breathe only through his mouth. Although this is not a major problem, it can be alarming and should always be investigated by the owner. There can be other reasons for such puffing; for example, a grass seed could be lodged in the dog's nasal cavity and would, of course, have to be removed at once.

Because the Shih Tzu is a reasonably long-backed breed, you should always be on the alert for possible back problems, especially in a dog's later years. In an ideal world, Shih Tzu should not be allowed to jump off furniture, although that is easier said than done! At any sign of spinal injury, a vet should be contacted without

delay, for in some cases even complete recovery can be achieved. Unfortunately, often partial paralysis results from spinal injury in Shih Tzu, but there are options to help affected dogs. An owner can choose to have his dog fitted with a little cart-like device to support the dog's paralyzed hind legs. Obviously, this is a serious decision to make and all of the options, however distressful, must be discussed openly with your family and vet.

Heart disease has been cited with reasonable frequency in the Shih Tzu, and this is not just limited to older dogs. However, there are many forms of heart disease and by no means are all

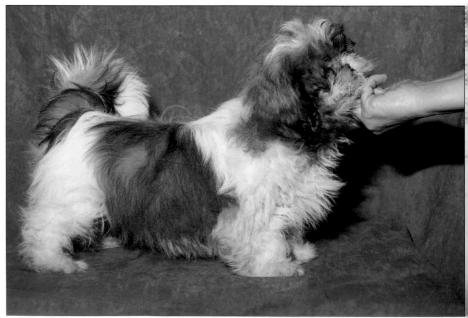

Potential Shih Tzu owners must be aware of the health problems that exist in the breed. An honorable breeder will have all dogs thoroughly checked for possible problems *before* breeding.

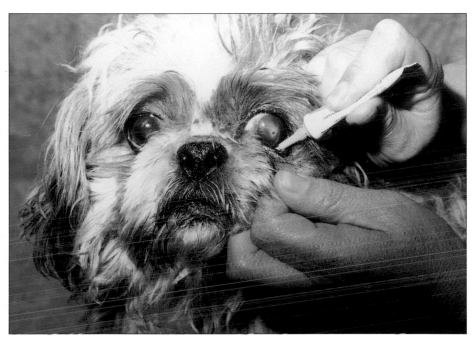

Because of the delicate nature of the Shih Tzu's large eyes, they are prone to injury. Seek veterinary assistance immediately in such circumstances.

inherited. Obviously, any sign of such disease should be checked out thoroughly by a vet, but it should be noted that many Shih Tzu live to a ripe old age with no heart problems at all.

CHINESE COAT BELIEFS

China's Madam Lee considered Shih Tzu with stiff coats to be comparatively more pugnacious and aggressive than those with thick woollen undercoats, the latter generally being of a milder, gentler nature. The Chinese described the Shih Tzu's coat using images such as "tassel-like," like a "waterfall" and like "petals of garlic."

Because of the breed's fairly prominent eyes, it is easier for a Shih Tzu to damage his eyes than it is for some other breeds. An ulcer on the eye may be caused by a scratch or a knock that may have gone unnoticed. At the first sign of eye trouble, a vet should be contacted because early treatment increases the chance of complete recovery. Eye problems, even those that seem small, could result in impaired vision or even loss of sight if left untreated. Reasonable care should be taken to avoid damage to the Shih Tzu's eyes, especially considering that no protection is provided when the dog's hair is tied back.

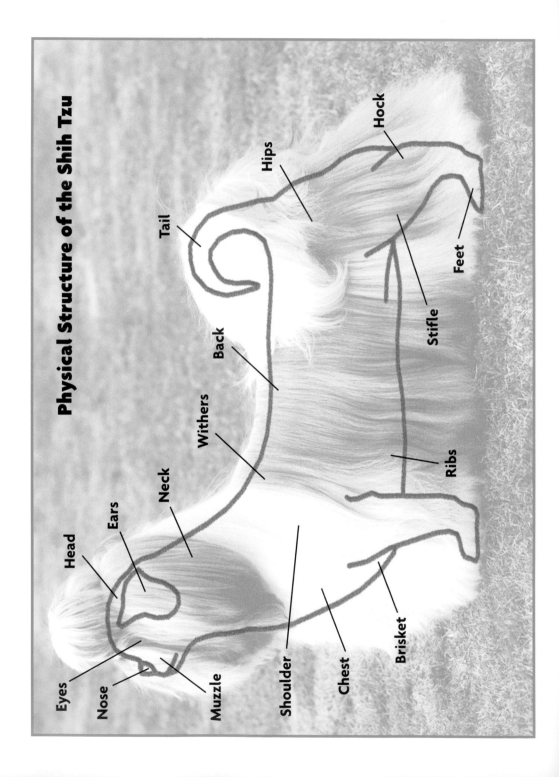

Physical Structure of the Shih Tzu

Tail

Hips

Hock

Feet

Stifle

Back

Ribs

Withers

Neck

Ears

Head

Eyes

Nose

Muzzle

Shoulder

Chest

Brisket

Shih Tzu

The breed standard for the Shih Tzu is effectively a "blueprint" for the breed. It sets down the various points of the dog in words, enabling a visual picture to be conjured up in the mind of the reader. However, this is more easily said than done. Not only do standards vary from country to country, but people's interpretations of breed standards vary also. It is this difference of interpretation which makes judges select different dogs for top honors, for their opinions differ as to which dog most closely fits the breed standard. That is not to say that a good dog does not win regularly under different judges, nor that an inferior dog may rarely even be placed at a show, at least not among quality competition.

COMMENTS
ON THE STANDARD
The Shih Tzu's breed standard is fairly self-explanatory, but readers interested in showing their Shih Tzu should learn as much as possible from established breeders and exhibitors. It is sensible to attend judges' seminars, often hosted by breed clubs, where the finer points of the breed can be explained fully and discussed.

There are, however, a few points of the standard that benefit from further elaboration here.

The nose of the Shih Tzu should be level or slightly tip-tilted. This means that when you look at the head in profile, the nose should be roughly in line with the lower eye rim. It may be tilted slightly upward, but it is highly untypical for it to be tilted downward. The stop, which is pronounced in this breed, is the area of indentation between the eyes where the nasal bone and skull meet. Proportionately, the ratio of the tip of nose to stop versus the stop to back of skull (occiput) should be 1 to 4 (or 5).

Most Shih Tzu have slightly undershot mouths, meaning that the lower incisors are positioned slightly forward of the upper. Clearly, a scissors or overshot bite is incorrect. Missing teeth in the Shih Tzu are not heavily penalized, for in the standard the usual requirement for full dentition is not specified. However, breeders should always bear in mind that missing incisors can all too easily lead to a narrowing of the jaw, and that the Shih Tzu's muzzle should be of ample width.

Head studies, showing correct structure and type and two different topknot styles.

There should be a clear distinction between dogs and bitches, especially evident in the head. A bitch has a distinctly feminine expression, while the head of the male is rather larger and more masculine in appearance.

Something that should be common to all Shih Tzu is that the breed is surprisingly heavy for its size, so that when picked up in your arms the weight of the dog can give you quite a surprise!

In profile, showing proper balance, structure and type with a mature coat and topknot as presented in the show ring.

The underline of the Shih Tzu is generally parallel with the line of the back, with no accentuated tuck-up, which would be untypical of the breed. When viewing the hind legs from the rear, they should be straight; the hocks should turn neither in nor out.

Movement of the Shih Tzu has been beautifully described as being like a ship in full sail. Indeed, movement displays the breed's arrogance, and the strong rear action shows the full pad of the hind feet as the dog moves away. This should be quite different from the typical movement of a Lhasa Apso, in which only a third of the pad should be seen. Provided that construction is correct, a Shih Tzu should be able to move with his head held high, without any necessity for the dog to be strung up by his lead. The high-set tail balances with the head and makes for a most attractive overall picture.

THE AMERICAN KENNEL CLUB STANDARD FOR THE SHIH TZU

General Appearance: The Shih Tzu is a sturdy, lively, alert toy dog with long flowing double coat. Befitting his noble Chinese ancestry as a highly valued, prized companion and palace pet, the Shih Tzu is proud of bearing, has a distinctively arrogant carriage with head well up and tail curved over the back. Although there has always been considerable size variation, the Shih Tzu must be compact, solid, carrying good weight and substance.

Even though a toy dog, the Shih Tzu must be subject to the

A variety of topknot styles are seen in the show ring. The upper left drawing is a puppy, while the others are all mature dogs.

same requirements of soundness and structure prescribed for all breeds, and any deviation from the ideal described in the standard should be penalized to the extent of the deviation. Structural faults common to all breeds are as undesirable in the Shih Tzu as in any other breed, regardless of whether or not such faults are specifically mentioned in the standard.

SIZE, PROPORTION AND SUBSTANCE
Size: Ideally, height at withers is 9 to 10.5 inches; but, not less than 8 inches nor more than 11 inches. Ideally, weight of mature dogs, 9 to 16 pounds. **Proportion:** Length between withers and root of tail is slightly longer than height at withers. The Shih Tzu must never be so high stationed as to appear leggy,

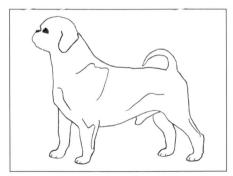

Top: Uncoated dog of correct balance and structure. Bottom: Uncoated dog showing faults in the breed: lacking sufficient neck; long-backed; high in rear with low-set kinked tail; lacking angulation at both ends; toes out in front due to crooked front legs.

nor so low stationed as to appear dumpy or squatty. **Substance:** Regardless of size, the Shih Tzu is always compact, solid and carries good weight and substance.

HEAD

Head: Round, broad, wide between eyes, its size in balance with the overall size of dog being neither too large nor too small. **Fault:** Narrow head, close-set eyes. **Expression:** Warm, sweet, wide-eyed, friendly and trusting. An overall well-balanced and pleasant expression supersedes the importance of individual parts. Care should be taken to look and examine well beyond the hair to determine if what is seen is the actual head and expression rather than an image created by grooming technique. **Eyes:** Large, round, not prominent, placed well apart, looking straight ahead. Very dark. Lighter on liver pigmented dogs and blue pigmented dogs. **Fault:** Small, close-set or light eyes; excessive eye white. **Ears:** Large, set slightly below crown of skull; heavily coated. **Skull:** Domed. **Stop:** There is a definite stop. **Muzzle:** Square, short, unwrinkled, with good cushioning, set no lower than bottom eye rim; never downturned. Ideally, no longer than 1 inch from tip of nose to stop, although length may vary slightly in relation to overall size of dog. Front of muzzle should be flat; lower lip and chin not protruding and definitely never

The side view of the Shih Tzu should not be square. The length is greater than the height.

receding. **Fault:** Snipiness, lack of definite stop. **Nose:** Nostrils are broad, wide, and open. **Pigmentation:** Nose, lips, eye rims are black on all colors, except liver on liver pigmented dogs and blue on blue pigmented dogs. **Fault:** Pink on nose, lips, or eye rims. **Bite:** Undershot. Jaw is broad and wide. A missing tooth or slightly misaligned teeth should not be too

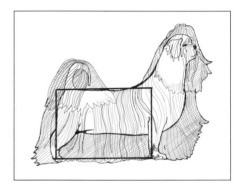

severely penalized. Teeth and tongue should not show when mouth is closed. **Fault:** Overshot bite.

NECK, TOPLINE, BODY

Of utmost importance is an overall well-balanced dog with no exaggerated features. **Neck:** Well set-on flowing smoothly into shoulders; of sufficient length to permit natural high head carriage and in balance with height and length of dog. **Topline:** Level. **Body:** Short-coupled and sturdy with no waist or tuck-up. The Shih Tzu is slightly longer than tall. **Fault:** Legginess.

Chest: Broad and deep with good spring-of-rib, however, not barrel-chested. Depth of rib cage should extend to just below elbow. Distance from elbow to withers is a little greater than from elbow to ground. **Croup:** Flat. **Tail:** Set on high, heavily plumed, carried in curve well over back. Too loose, too tight, too flat, or too low set a tail is undesirable and should be penalized to extent of deviation.

FOREQUARTERS

Shoulders: Well-angulated, well laid-back, well laid-in, fitting smoothly into body. **Legs:** Straight, well-boned, muscular, set well-apart and under chest, with elbows set close to body. **Pasterns:** Strong, perpendicular. **Dewclaws:** May be removed. **Feet:** Firm, well-padded, point straight ahead.

HINDQUARTERS

Angulation of hindquarters should be in balance with forequarters. **Legs:** Well-boned, muscular, and straight when viewed from rear with well-bent stifles, not close set but in line with forequarters. **Hocks:** Well let down, perpendicular. Fault: Hyperextension of hocks. **Dewclaws:** May be removed. **Feet:** Firm, well-padded, point straight ahead.

COAT

Coat: Luxurious, double-coated, dense, long, and flowing. Slight wave permissible. Hair on top of

head is tied up. **Fault:** Sparse coat, single coat, curly coat. **Trimming:** Feet, bottom of coat, and anus may be done for neatness and to facilitate movement. **Fault:** Excessive trimming.

The Shih Tzu's proper gait should be smooth, flowing, with front legs reaching well forward, and strong rear action.

COLOR AND MARKINGS

All are permissible and to be considered equally.

GAIT

The Shih Tzu moves straight and must be shown at its own natural speed, neither raced nor strung-up, to evaluate its smooth, flowing, effortless movement with good front reach and equally strong rear drive, level topline, naturally high head carriage, and tail carried in gentle curve over back.

TEMPERAMENT

As the sole purpose of the Shih Tzu is that of a companion and house pet, it is essential that its temperament be outgoing, happy, affectionate, friendly and trusting towards all.

Shih Tzu

You have probably decided on a Shih Tzu as your pet of choice following a visit to the home of a friend or acquaintance, where you saw an adorable Shih Tzu wandering happily around the house and joining politely in the family fun. However, as a potential new owner, you must realize that a good deal of care, commitment and careful training goes into raising a boisterous puppy so that your pet turns into a well-behaved adult.

In deciding to take on a Shih Tzu puppy, you will be committing yourself to around 14 years of responsibility. No dog should be discarded after a few months, or even a few years, after the novelty has worn off. Instead, your Shih Tzu should be joining your house-

ARE YOU PREPARED?

Unfortunately, when a puppy is bought by someone who does not take into consideration the time and attention that dog ownership requires, it is the puppy who suffers when he is either abandoned or placed in a shelter by a frustrated owner. So all of the "homework" you do in preparation for your pup's arrival will benefit you both. The more informed you are, the more you will know what to expect and the better equipped you will be to handle the ups and downs of raising a puppy. Hopefully, everyone in the household is willing to do his part in raising and caring for the pup. The anticipation of owning a dog often brings a lot of promises from excited family members: "I will walk him every day," "I will feed him," "I will house-train him," etc., but these things take time and effort, and promises can easily be forgotten once the novelty of the new pet has worn off.

Keep in mind that when you take your Shih Tzu puppy home, you are making a 14-year commitment. Be certain that everyone in your household wants to live with a dog.

A vital part of the socialization of any puppy is meeting young people. The Shih Tzu pup welcomes the advances of well-behaved children, but supervision is always necessary with such a small puppy.

hold to spend the rest of his days with you.

Although temperamentally a Shih Tzu is much easier to look after than many other breeds, you will still need to carry out a certain amount of training. Unlike some larger dogs, the Shih Tzu will not respond well to overly strict training. Instead, you will need to take a firm but gentle approach in order to get the very best out of your pet.

A Shih Tzu generally likes to be clean around the house, but you will need to teach your puppy what is and is not expected. You will need to be consistent in your instructions; it is no good accepting certain

behavior one day and not the next. Not only will your puppy simply not understand, he will be utterly confused. Your Shih Tzu will want to please you, so you will need to demonstrate clearly and consistently to your puppy what behavior is acceptable.

BUYER BEWARE
When breeds become very popular, and such is the case with the Shih Tzu, although there are many truly dedicated breeders, there become an increasing number of less reputable ones, too. It is therefore essential to select a breeder with the very greatest of care.

Your Shih Tzu will be fairly small, and therefore probably less troublesome than a large dog, but there will undoubtedly be a period of settling in. This will be great fun, but you must be prepared for mishaps around the home during the first few weeks of your life together. It will be important that your breakable possessions are kept well out of harm's (meaning the puppy's) way, and you will have to think twice about where you place hot cups of coffee or anything break- able. Accidents can and do happen, so you will need to think ahead so as to avoid them. Electrical cords must be carefully concealed, and your puppy must be taught

TEMPERAMENT COUNTS

Your selection of a good puppy can be determined by your needs. A show potential or a good pet? It is your choice. Every puppy, however, should be of good temperament. Although show-quality puppies are bred and raised with emphasis on physical conformation, responsible breeders strive for equally good temperament. Do not buy from a breeder who concentrates solely on physical beauty at the expense of personality.

where he can go and where he cannot go.

Before making your commit- ment to a new puppy, do also think carefully about your future vacation plans. Depending on where you wish to travel, your dog may or may not be able to travel with you. If you have thought things through carefully and discussed the matter thor- oughly with all members of your family, hopefully you will have come to the right decision. If you decide that a Shih Tzu should join your family, this will hope- fully be a happy, long-term rela- tionship for all parties concerned.

BUYING A SHIH TZU PUPPY

Although you may be looking for a Shih Tzu as a pet dog rather than as a show dog, this does not mean that you want a dog that is in any way "second-rate." A caring breeder will have brought up the entire litter of puppies with the same amount of dedica- tion, and a puppy destined for a pet home should be just as healthy as one that hopes to end up in the show ring.

Because you have carefully selected this breed, you will want a Shih Tzu that is a typical speci- men, both in looks and in temperament. In your endeavors to find such a puppy, you will have to select the breeder with care. The American Kennel Club will almost certainly be able to

Responsible breeders select only top-rate Shih Tzu for breeding in order to perpetuate the best in health, temperament and soundness.

give you names of breeders or other contacts within Shih Tzu breed clubs. These people can possibly put you in touch with breeders who may have puppies for sale. However, although they can point you in the right direction, it will be up to you to do your homework carefully.

Even though you are probably not looking for a show dog, it is always a good idea to visit a show so that you can see quality specimens of the breed. This will also give you an opportunity to meet breeders who will probably be able to answer some of your queries. In addition, you will get some idea about which breeders appear to take most care of their stock and which are likely to have

given their puppies the best possible start in life. Something else you may be able to decide upon is which color appeals to you most, although this is purely personal preference.

PUPPY APPEARANCE
Your puppy should have a well-fed appearance but not a distended abdomen, which may indicate worms or incorrect feeding, or both. The body should be firm, with a solid feel. The skin of the abdomen should be pale pink and clean, without signs of scratching or rash. Check the hind legs to see if the dewclaws were removed, as many Shih Tzu breeders have this done.

When buying your puppy, you will need to know about vaccinations: which ones have been given already and which ones the puppy still needs. It is important that any injections already given by a veterinarian have been recorded and documented for proof. A worming routine is also vital for any young puppy, so the breeder should be able to tell you exactly what treatment has been given, when it was administered and how you should continue.

Clearly, when selecting a puppy, the one you choose must be in good condition. The coat should look healthy and there should be no discharge from the eyes or nose. Ears should also be clean and, of course, there should be absolutely no sign of parasites. Check that the skin is healthy and free of rashes and irritations. Of course, the puppy you choose should not have any evidence of loose stool.

As in several other breeds, some Shih Tzu puppies have umbilical hernias, which can be

PEDIGREE VS. REGISTRATION CERTIFICATE

Too often new owners are confused between these two important documents. Your puppy's pedigree, essentially a family tree, is a written record of a dog's genealogy of three generations or more. The pedigree will show you the names as well as performance titles of all the dogs in your pup's background. Your breeder must provide you with a registration application, with his part properly filled out. You must complete the application and send it to the AKC with the proper fee. The seller must provide you with complete records to identify the puppy. The AKC requires that the seller provide the buyer with the following: breed; sex, color and markings; date of birth; litter number (when available); names and registration numbers of the parents; breeder's name; and date sold or delivered.

seen as a small lump on the tummy where the umbilical cord was attached. It is preferable not to have such a hernia on any puppy, but you should check for this at the outset. If a hernia is present, you should discuss its seriousness with the breeder. Most umbilical hernias are safe, but your vet should keep an eye on it in case an operation is needed.

Just a few words of warning: Be very careful about where you purchase your puppy. Find your breeder through a reputable source, like a breed club, and visit

A ten-day-old Shih Tzu puppy with his eyes just opened. Toy-breed puppies should be about 12 weeks old before they leave for new homes.

PET INSURANCE

Just like you can insure your car, your house and your own health, you likewise can insure your dog's health. Investigate a pet insurance policy by talking to your vet. Depending on the age of your dog, the breed and the kind of coverage you desire, your policy can be very affordable. Most policies cover accidental injuries, poisoning and thousands of medical problems and illnesses, including cancers. Some carriers also offer routine care and immunization coverage, including heartworm preventative, prescription flea control, annual checkups, teeth cleaning, spaying/neutering, health screening and more. These policies are more costly than more basic ones, but may be well worth the investment.

You can visit a breeder and choose your puppy even before he is ready to leave his mother. Ideally you will be able to meet the dam of your puppy to get a good idea of the temperament and other attributes.

43

TIME TO GO HOME

Breeders rarely release puppies until they are eight to ten weeks of age. This is an acceptable age for most breeds of dog, excepting toy breeds, which are not released until around 12 weeks, given their petite sizes. If a breeder has a puppy that is 12 weeks of age or older, he is likely well socialized and house-trained. Be sure that it is otherwise healthy before deciding to take him home.

the quarters in which the pups are kept. Always insist that you see the puppy's dam and, if possible, the sire. While frequently the sire will not be owned by the litter's breeder, a photograph may be available for you to see. Ask if the breeder has any other of the puppy's relatives that you can meet. For example, there may be an older half-sister or half-brother, and it would be interesting for you to see how they have turned out: their size, coat quality, temperament and so on.

Be sure, too, that if you decide to buy a puppy, all relevant documentation is provided at the time of sale. You will need a copy of the pedigree, AKC registration certificate, vaccination records and worming records, and a

A newly born Shih Tzu puppy, only 24 hours old. His eyes are still closed.

feeding chart so that you know exactly how the puppy has been fed and how you should continue. Some thoughtful breeders provide their puppy buyers with a small amount of food. This prevents the risk of an upset tummy, allowing for a gradual change of diet if that particular brand of food is not locally available.

COMMITMENT OF OWNERSHIP

After considering all of these factors, you have already made some very important decisions about selecting your puppy. You have chosen the Shih Tzu, which means that you have decided which characteristics you want in a dog and what type of dog will best fit into your family and lifestyle. If you have selected a breeder, you have gone a step further—you have done your research and found a responsible, conscientious person who breeds

Spend as much time observing the puppies as possible. Often the juvenile personality gives a preview of the adult temperament. You should also decide if you'd prefer a male or a female.

quality Shih Tzu and who should be a reliable source of help as you and your puppy adjust to life together. If you have observed a litter in action, you have obtained a firsthand look at the dynamics of a puppy "pack" and, thus, you should learn about each pup's individual personality—perhaps you have even found one that particularly appeals to you.

However, even if you have not yet found the Shih Tzu puppy of your dreams, observing pups will help you learn to recognize certain behavior and to determine what a pup's behavior indicates about his temperament. You will be able to pick out which pups are the leaders, which ones are less outgoing, which ones are confident, which ones are shy, playful, friendly, aggressive, etc. Equally as important, you will learn to recognize what a healthy pup should look and act like. All

YOUR SCHEDULE . . .
If you lead an erratic, unpredictable life, with daily or weekly changes in your work requirements, consider the problems of owning a puppy. The new puppy has to be fed regularly, socialized (loved, petted, handled, introduced to other people) and, most importantly, allowed to go outdoors for house-training. As the dog gets older, he can be more tolerant of deviations in his feeding and relief schedule.

of these things will help you in your search, and when you find the Shih Tzu that was meant for you, you will know it!

Researching your breed, selecting a responsible breeder and observing as many pups as possible are all important steps on the way to dog ownership. It may seem like a lot of effort…and you have not even brought the pup home yet! Remember, though, you cannot be too careful when it comes to deciding on the type of dog you want and finding out about your prospective pup's background. Buying a puppy is not—or should not be—just another whimsical purchase. This is one instance in which you actually do get to choose your own family! You may be thinking that buying a puppy should be fun—it should not be so serious and so much work. Keep in mind that your puppy is not a cuddly stuffed

QUALITY FOOD
The cost of food must be mentioned. All dogs need a good-quality food with an adequate supply of protein to develop their bones and muscles properly. Most dogs are not picky eaters but, unless fed properly, can quickly succumb to skin problems.

toy or lawn sculpture, but a creature that will become a real member of your family. You will come to realize that, while buying a puppy is a pleasurable and exciting endeavor, it is not something to be taken lightly. Relax…the fun will start when the pup comes home!

Always keep in mind that a puppy is nothing more than a baby in a furry disguise…a baby who is virtually helpless in a human world and who trusts his owner for fulfillment of his basic needs for survival. In addition to food, water and shelter, your pup needs care, protection, guidance and love. If you are not prepared to commit to this, then you are not prepared to own a dog.

"Wait a minute," you say. "How hard could this be? All of my neighbors own dogs and they seem to be doing just fine. Why should I have to worry about all of this?" Well, you should not worry about it; in fact, you will probably find that once your Shih Tzu pup gets used to his new home, he will fall into his place in the family quite naturally. But it never hurts to emphasize the commitment of dog ownership. With some time and patience, it is really not too difficult to raise a curious and exuberant Shih Tzu pup to become a well-adjusted and well-mannered adult dog—a dog that could be your most loyal friend.

PREPARING PUPPY'S PLACE IN YOUR HOME

Researching your breed and finding a breeder are only two aspects of the "homework" you will have to do before bringing your Shih Tzu puppy home. You will also have to prepare your home and family for the new addition. Much as you would prepare a nursery for a newborn baby, you will need to designate a place in your home that will be the puppy's own. How you prepare your home will depend on how much freedom the dog will be allowed. Whatever you decide, you must ensure that he has a place that he can "call his own."

When you bring your new puppy into your home, you are bringing him into what will become his home as well. Obviously, you did not buy a puppy so that he could take over your house, but in order for a puppy to grow into a stable, well-adjusted dog, he has to feel comfortable in his surroundings. Remember, he is leaving the warmth and security of his dam and littermates, as well as the familiarity of the only place he has ever known, so it is important to make his transition as easy as possible. By preparing a place in your home for the puppy, you are making him feel as welcome as possible in a strange new place. It should not take him long to get used to it, but the sudden shock

of being transplanted is somewhat traumatic for a young pup. Imagine how a small child would feel in the same situation—that is how your puppy must be feeling. It is up to you to reassure him and to let him know, "Little fellow, you are going to like it here!"

When you bring your new puppy home, you must be prepared. You'll need a crate, food, toys, collar and lead, food and water bowls, bedding and perhaps other items that your vet might suggest.

WHAT YOU SHOULD BUY
CRATE

To someone unfamiliar with the use of crates in dog training, it may seem like punishment to shut a dog in a crate, but this is not the case at all. Most breeders and trainers recommend crates as the preferred tool for pet puppies as well as show puppies. Crates are not cruel—crates have many humane and highly effective uses in dog care and training. For example, crate

47

Photo Courtesy of Doskocil

A medium-size crate is suitable for the puppy or full-grown Shih Tzu.

serves as a "doggie bedroom" of sorts—your Shih Tzu can curl up in his crate when he wants to sleep or when he just needs a break. Many dogs sleep in their crates overnight. When lined with soft bedding and with his favorite toy, a crate becomes a cozy pseudo-den for your dog. Like his ancestors, he too will seek out the comfort and retreat of a den—you just happen to be providing him with something a little more luxurious than what his early ancestors enjoyed.

CRATE-TRAINING TIPS

During crate training, you should partition off the section of the crate in which the pup stays. If he is given too big an area, this will hinder your training efforts. Crate training is based on the fact that a dog does not like to soil his sleeping quarters, so it is ineffective to keep a pup in a crate that is so big that he can eliminate in one end and get far enough away from it to sleep. Also, you want to make the crate den-like for the pup. Blankets and a favorite toy will make the crate cozy for the small pup; as he grows, you may want to evict some of his "roommates" to make more room. It will take some coaxing at first, but be patient. Given some time to get used to it, your pup will adapt to his new home-within-a-home quite nicely.

training is a very popular and very successful housebreaking method. A crate can keep your dog safe during travel and, perhaps most importantly, a crate provides your dog with a place of his own in your home. It

As far as purchasing a crate, the type that you buy is up to you. It will most likely be one of the two most popular types: wire or fiberglass. There are advantages and disadvantages to each type. For example, a wire crate is more open, allowing the air to flow through and affording the dog a view of what is going on around him, while a fiberglass crate is sturdier. Both can double as travel crates, providing protection for the dog. The size of the crate is another thing to consider. Puppies do not stay puppies forever—in fact, sometimes it seems as if they grow right before your eyes. A Shih Tzu does not grow to be a large dog, but he is a substantial dog for his height, which can be up to 11 inches. Make sure that the crate you choose will accommodate your Shih Tzu both as a pup and as a full-grown dog.

BEDDING

A nice crate pad in the dog's crate will help the dog feel more at home and you may also like to give him a small blanket. This bedding will take the place of the leaves, twigs, etc., that the pup would use in the wild to make a den; the pup can make his own "burrow" in the crate. Although your pup is far removed from his den-making ancestors, the denning instinct is still a part of his genetic makeup. Also, until you bring your pup home, he has

been sleeping amid the warmth of his mother and littermates, and while a blanket is not the same as a warm, breathing body, it still provides heat and something with which to snuggle. You will want to wash your pup's bedding frequently in case he has an accident in his crate, and replace or remove any blanket that becomes ragged and starts to fall apart.

TOYS

Toys are a must for dogs of all ages, especially for curious playful pups. Puppies are the "chil-

The crate you buy for your Shih Tzu will become his home inside your home.

dren" of the dog world, and what child does not love toys? Chew toys provide enjoyment to both dog and owner—your dog will enjoy playing with his favorite toys, while you will enjoy the fact that they distract him from your expensive shoes and leather sofa. Puppies love to chew; in fact, chewing is a physical need for pups as they are teething, and everything looks appetizing! The full range of your possessions—from wash cloth and gloves to Oriental rug—are fair game in the eyes of a teething pup. Puppies are not all that discerning when it comes to finding something to literally "sink their teeth into"—everything tastes great!

Shih Tzu puppies are not very aggressive chewers, but only the safest toys should be offered to them. Breeders advise owners to resist stuffed toys, because they can become de-stuffed in no time. The overly excited pup may ingest the stuffing, which is neither digestible nor nutritious.

Similarly, squeaky toys are quite popular, but only under your supervision. Perhaps a squeaky toy can be used as an aid in training, but not for free play. If a pup "disembowels" one of these, the small plastic squeaker inside can be dangerous if swallowed. Monitor the condition of all your pup's toys carefully and get rid of any that have been

Only offer your puppy toys that have been especially made for dogs. Children's toys are often too soft for the sharp teeth of Shih Tzu puppies.

chewed to the point of becoming potentially dangerous.

Be careful of natural bones, which have a tendency to splinter into sharp, dangerous pieces. Also be careful of rawhide, which can turn into pieces that are easy to swallow or into a mushy mess on your carpet.

LEAD

A nylon lead is probably the best option as it is the most resistant to puppy teeth should your pup take a liking to chewing on his lead. Of course, this is a habit that should be nipped in the bud, but if your pup likes to chew on his lead he has a very slim chance of being able to chew through the strong nylon. Nylon leads are also lightweight, which is good for a young Shih Tzu who is just getting used to the idea of walking on a lead. For everyday walking and safety purposes, the nylon lead is a good choice. As your pup grows up and gets used to walking on the lead, you may want to purchase a flexible lead. These leads allow you to extend the length to give the dog a broader area to explore or to shorten the length to keep the dog close to you. Of course there are special thin leads for showing purposes, but these are not safe enough for routine walks.

COLLAR

Your pup should get used to wearing a collar all the time since you

PHOTO BY MIKKI PET PRODUCTS

TOYS, TOYS, TOYS!

With a big variety of dog toys available, and so many that look like they would be a lot of fun for a dog, be careful in your selection. It is amazing what a set of puppy teeth can do to an innocent-looking toy; so, obviously, safety is a major consideration. Be sure to choose the most durable products that you can find. Hard nylon bones and toys are a safe bet, and many of them are offered in different scents and flavors that will be sure to capture your dog's attention. It is always fun to play a game of catch with your dog, and there are balls and flying discs that are specially made to withstand dog teeth.

will want to attach his ID tags to it. You have to attach the lead to something! A lightweight nylon collar is a good choice; make sure that it fits snugly enough so that

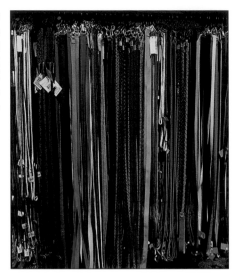

Pet shops usually stock a wide assortment of leads. Shih Tzu puppies only need light, nylon leads.

danger of being chewed by puppy teeth and you do not want your dog to be constantly chewing apart his bowl (for his safety and for your purse!).

CLEANING SUPPLIES

Until a pup is house-trained, you will be doing a lot of cleaning. Accidents will occur, which is okay in the beginning because the puppy does not know any better. All you can do is be prepared to clean up any accidents. Old rags, towels, newspapers and a safe disinfectant are good to have on hand.

BEYOND THE BASICS

The items previously discussed are the bare necessities. You will find out what else you need as

the pup cannot wriggle out of it, but is loose enough so that it will not be uncomfortably tight around the pup's neck. You should be able to fit a finger between the pup and the collar. It may take some time for your pup to get used to wearing the collar, but soon he will not even notice that it is there.

FOOD AND WATER BOWLS

Your pup will need two bowls, one for food and one for water. You may want two sets of bowls, one for inside and one for outside, depending on where the dog will be spending time. Stainless steel or sturdy plastic bowls are popular choices. Plastic bowls are more chewable. Dogs tend not to chew on the steel variety, which can be sterilized. It is important to buy sturdy bowls since anything is in

FINANCIAL RESPONSIBILITY

Grooming tools, collars, leashes, a crate, a dog bed and, of course, toys will be expenses to you when you first obtain your pup, and the cost will continue throughout your dog's lifetime. If your puppy damages or destroys your possessions (as most puppies surely will!) or something belonging to a neighbor, you can calculate additional expense. There is also flea and pest control, which every dog owner faces more than once. You must be able to handle the financial responsibility of owning a dog.

Choose the Appropriate Collar

The **BUCKLE COLLAR** is the standard collar used for everyday purposes. Be sure that you adjust the buckle on growing puppies. Check it every day. It can become too tight overnight! These collars can be made of leather or nylon. Attach your dog's identification tags to this collar.

The **CHOKE COLLAR** is constructed of highly polished steel so that it slides easily through the stainless steel loop. The idea is that the dog controls the pressure around his neck and he will stop pulling if the collar becomes uncomfortable. It is used *only* for training and should *never* be left on a dog. The choke collar is not suitable for the Shih Tzu.

The **HALTER** is for a trained dog that has to be restrained to prevent running away, chasing a cat and the like. Considered the most humane of all collars, it is frequently used on smaller dogs on which collars are not comfortable.

Your local pet shop sells an array of dishes and bowls for water and food.

Photo by Mikki Pet Products

you go along—grooming supplies, flea/tick protection, baby gates to partition a room, etc. These things will vary depending on your situation but it is important that you have everything you need to feed and make your Shih Tzu comfortable in his first few days at home.

PUPPY-PROOFING YOUR HOME

Aside from making sure that your Shih Tzu will be comfortable in your home, you also have to make sure that your home is safe for your Shih Tzu. This means taking precautions that your pup will not get into anything he should not get into and that there is nothing within his reach that may harm him should he sniff it, chew it, inspect it, etc. This probably seems obvious since, while you are primarily concerned with your pup's safety, at the same time you do not want your belongings to be

SKULL & CROSSBONES

Thoroughly puppy-proof your house before bringing your puppy home. Never use cockroach or rodent poisons or plant fertilizers in any area accessible to the puppy. Avoid the use of toilet cleaners. Most dogs are born with "toilet-bowl sonar" and will take a drink if the lid is left open. Also keep the trash secured and out of reach.

ruined. Breakables should be placed out of reach if your dog is to have full run of the house. If he is to be limited to certain places within the house, keep any potentially dangerous items in the "off-limits" areas. An electrical cord can pose a danger should the puppy decide to taste it—and who is going to convince a pup that it would not make a great chew toy? Cords should be fastened tightly against the wall. If your dog is going to spend time in a crate, make sure that there is nothing near his crate that he can reach if he sticks his curious little paws through the openings. Just as you would with a child, keep all household cleaners and chemicals where the pup cannot get to them.

It is also important to make sure that the outside of your home is safe. Of course your puppy should never be unsupervised, but a pup let loose in the yard will want to run and explore, and he should be granted that freedom. Do not let a fence give you a false sense of security; you would be surprised how crafty (and persistent) a dog can be in figuring out how to dig under and squeeze his way through small holes, or to jump or climb over a fence. The remedy is to make the fence high enough so that it really is impossible for your dog to get over it (about 4 feet should suffice), and well embedded into the ground. Check the fence periodically to

It is your responsibility to clean up after your dog has relieved himself. Pet shops have various aids to assist in the cleanup job.

ensure that it is in good shape and make repairs as needed; a very determined pup may return to the same spot to "work on it" until he is able to get through.

FIRST TRIP TO THE VET
You have picked out your puppy, and your home and family are ready. Now all you have to do is

> **NATURAL TOXINS**
> Examine your lawn and home landscaping before bringing your puppy home. Many varieties of plants have leaves, stems or flowers that are toxic if ingested, and you can depend on a curious puppy to investigate them. Ask your vet for information on poisonous plants or research them at your library.

collect your Shih Tzu from the breeder and the fun begins, right? Well...not so fast. Something else you need to prepare is your pup's first trip to the veterinarian. Perhaps the breeder can recommend someone in the area who specializes in Shih Tzu, or maybe you know some other Shih Tzu owners who can suggest a good vet. Either way, you should have an appointment arranged for your

Raising a Shih Tzu puppy is a life experience for a young person, and the dog will grow up to treat his young master as a sibling to be loved and trusted.

pup before you pick him up and plan on taking him for an examination before bringing him home.

The pup's first visit will consist of an overall examination to make sure that the pup does not have any problems that are not apparent. The veterinarian will also set up a schedule for the pup's vaccinations; the breeder will inform you of which ones the pup has already received and the vet can continue from there.

INTRODUCTION TO THE FAMILY

Everyone in the house will be excited about the puppy's coming home and will want to pet him and play with him, but it is best to make the introduction low-key so as not to overwhelm the puppy. He is apprehensive already. It is the first time he has been separated from his mother and the breeder, and the ride to your home is likely the first time he

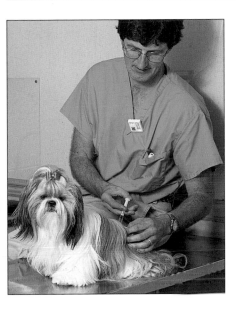

gently. He definitely needs human attention and he needs to be touched—this is how to form an immediate bond. Just remember that the pup is experiencing a lot of things for the first time, at the same time. There are new people, new noises, new smells and new things to investigate, so be gentle, be affectionate and be as comforting as you can be.

YOUR PUP'S FIRST NIGHT HOME

You have traveled home with your new charge safely in his crate. He's been to the vet for a thorough checkup; he's been weighed, his papers examined, perhaps he's even been vaccinated and wormed as well. He's met the family and licked the whole family, including the

You should have your dog examined regularly by your veterinarian. Your adult Shih Tzu's booster vaccinations should coincide with his physical examination.

has been in a car. The last thing you want to do is smother him, as this will only frighten him further. This is not to say that human contact is not extremely necessary at this stage, because this is the time when a connection between the pup and his human family is formed. Gentle petting and soothing words should help console him, as well as just putting him down and letting him explore on his own (under your watchful eye, of course).

The pup may approach the family members or may busy himself with exploring for a while. Gradually, each person should spend some time with the pup, one at a time, crouching down to get as close to the pup's level as possible and letting him sniff their hands and petting him

PUPPY FEEDING
You will probably start feeding your pup the same food that he has been getting from the breeder; the breeder may give you a few days' supply to start you off. Although you should not give your pup too many treats, you will want to have puppy treats on hand for coaxing, training, rewards, etc. Be careful, though, as a small pup's calorie requirements are relatively low and a few treats can add up to almost a full day's worth of calories without the required nutrition.

TRAINING TIP

Training your puppy takes much patience and can be frustrating at times, but you should see results from your efforts. If you have a puppy that seems untrainable, take him to a trainer or behaviorist. The dog may have a personality problem that requires the help of a professional, or perhaps you need help in learning how to train your dog.

excited children and the less-than-happy cat. He's explored his area, his new bed, the yard and anywhere else he's been permit-

ted. He's eaten his first meal at home and relieved himself in the proper place. He's heard lots of new sounds, smelled new friends and seen more of the outside world than ever before.

That was just the first day! He's worn out and is ready for bed. . .or so you think!

It's puppy's first night and you are ready to say "Good night"—keep in mind that this is puppy's first night ever to be sleeping alone. His dam and littermates are no longer at paw's length and he's a bit scared, cold and lonely. Be reassuring to your new family member, but this is not the time to

The puppies have been socialized to their own brothers and sisters. The socialization process with people must continue as the puppy grows up.

spoil him and give in to his inevitable whining.

Puppies whine. They whine to let the others know where they are and hopefully to get company out of it. Place your pup in his new bed or crate in his room and close the door. Mercifully, he may fall asleep without a peep. When the inevitable occurs, ignore the whining: he is fine. Be strong and keep his interest in mind. Do not allow your heart to become guilty and visit the pup. He will fall asleep. . .eventually.

Many breeders recommend placing a piece of bedding from his former homestead in his new bed so that he recognizes the scent of his littermates. Others still advise placing a hot water bottle in his bed for warmth. This latter may be a good idea provided the pup doesn't attempt to suckle—he'll get good and wet and may not fall asleep so fast.

Puppy's first night can be stressful for the pup and his new family. Remember that you are setting the tone of nighttime at

your house. Unless you want to play with your pup every night at 10 p.m., midnight and 2 a.m., don't initiate the habit. Your family will thank you, and eventually so will your pup!

Don't overwhelm the puppy. Give your new Shih Tzu baby time to adjust to the family and activity of the household. Provide a cozy bed in which he can sleep or just take a break.

PREVENTING PUPPY PROBLEMS
SOCIALIZATION
Now that you have done all of the preparatory work and have helped your pup get accustomed to his new home and family, it is about time for you to have some fun! Socializing your Shih Tzu pup gives you the opportunity to show off your new friend, and your pup gets to reap the benefits of being an adorable chrysanthemum-faced baby that people will want to pet and, in general, think is absolutely precious!

Besides getting to know his new family, your puppy should be

IN DUE TIME
It will take at least two weeks for your puppy to become accustomed to his new surroundings. Give him lots of love, attention, handling, frequent opportunities to relieve himself, a diet he likes to eat and a place he can call his own.

DOG MEETS WORLD

Thorough socialization includes not only meeting new people but also being introduced to new experiences such as riding in the car, having his coat brushed, hearing the tv, walking in a crowd—the list is endless. The more your dog experiences, and the more positive the experiences are, the less of a shock and the less frightening it will be for him to encounter new things.

weeks is the most critical, as this is the time when he forms his impressions of the outside world. The interaction he receives during the socialization period time should be gentle and reassuring. Lack of socialization or negative experiences can manifest themselves in fear and aggression as the dog grows up. He needs lots of human contact, affection, handling and exposure to other animals.

Once your pup has received his necessary vaccinations, feel free to take him out and about (on his lead, of course). Walk him around the neighborhood, take him on your daily errands, let people pet him, let him meet other dogs and pets, etc. Puppies do not have to try to make friends; there will be no shortage of people who will want to introduce themselves. Just make sure that you carefully supervise each meeting. If the neighborhood children want to say hello, for example, that is great—children and pups most often make great companions. However, sometimes an excited child can unintentionally handle a pup too roughly, or an overzealous pup can playfully nip a little too hard. You want to make socialization experiences positive ones. What a pup learns during this very formative stage will impact his attitude toward future encounters. You want your dog to

exposed to other people, animals and situations, but of course he must not come into close contact with dogs you don't know well until his course of vaccinations is fully complete. This will help him become well adjusted as he grows up and less prone to being timid or fearful of the new things he will encounter. Your pup's socialization began at the breeder's but now it is your responsibility to continue it. The socialization he receives up until the age of 12

be comfortable around everyone. A pup that has a bad experience with a child may grow up to be a dog that is shy around or aggressive toward children.

CONSISTENCY IN TRAINING
Dogs, being pack animals, naturally need a leader, or else they try to establish dominance in their packs. When you bring a dog into your family, the choice of who becomes the leader and who becomes the "pack" is entirely up to you! Your pup's intuitive quest for dominance, coupled with the fact that it is nearly impossible to look at an adorable Shih Tzu pup, with his "puppy-dog" eyes and button nose, and not cave in, give the pup almost an unfair advantage in getting the upper hand! A pup will definitely test the waters to see what he can and cannot do. Do not give in to those pleading eyes—stand your ground when it comes to disciplining the pup and make sure that all family members do the same. It will only confuse the pup when Mother tells him to get off the couch when he is used to sitting up there with Father to watch the nightly news. Avoid discrepancies by having all members of the household decide on the rules before the pup even comes home...and be consistent in enforcing them! Early training shapes the dog's personality, so

you cannot be unclear in what you expect.

COMMON PUPPY PROBLEMS
The best way to prevent puppy problems is to be proactive in stopping an undesirable behavior as soon as it starts. The old saying "You can't teach an old dog new tricks" does not necessarily hold true, but it *is* true that it is much easier to discourage bad behavior in a young developing pup than to wait until the pup's bad behavior becomes the adult dog's bad habit. Let's now look at some problems that are especially prevalent in puppies as they develop.

NIPPING
As puppies start to teethe, they feel the need to sink their teeth into anything available...unfortunately, that includes your fingers, arms, hair and toes. You may find this behavior cute for the first five seconds...until you feel

---

MENTAL AND DENTAL
Toys not only help your puppy get the physical and mental stimulation he needs but also provide a great way to keep his teeth clean. Hard rubber or nylon toys, especially those constructed with grooves, are designed to scrape away plaque, preventing bad breath and gum infection.

calling out for attention to make sure that you know he is there and that you have not forgotten about him. He feels insecure when he is left alone, when you are out of the house and he is in

Young puppies, just a few days old, know how to whine and cry when they are hungry or uncomfortable. Puppies will try hard to tell you how they feel.

just how sharp those puppy teeth are. This is something you want to discourage immediately and consistently with a firm "No!" (or whatever number of firm "Nos" it takes for him to understand that you mean business). Then replace your finger with an appropriate chew toy. While this behavior is merely annoying when the dog is young, it can become dangerous as your Shih Tzu's adult teeth grow in and his jaws develop, and he continues to think it is okay to gnaw on human appendages. Your Shih Tzu does not mean any harm with a friendly nip, but he also does not know that his teeth can cause pain.

CRYING/WHINING

Your pup will often cry, whine, whimper, howl or make some type of commotion when he is left alone. This is basically his way of

---

CHEWING TIPS

Chewing goes hand in hand with nipping in the sense that a teething puppy is always looking for a way to soothe his aching gums. In this case, instead of chewing on you, he may have taken a liking to your favorite shoe or something else which he should not be chewing. Again, realize that this is a normal canine behavior that does not need to be discouraged, only redirected. Your pup just needs to be taught what is acceptable to chew on and what is off-limits. Consistently tell him "No" when you catch him chewing on something forbidden and give him a chew toy.

Conversely, praise him when you catch him chewing on something appropriate. In this way you are discouraging the inappropriate behavior and reinforcing the desired behavior. The puppy's chewing should stop after his adult teeth have come in, but an adult dog continues to chew for various reasons—perhaps because he is bored, needs to relieve tension or just likes to chew. That is why it is important to redirect his chewing when he is still young.

his crate or when you are in another part of the house and he cannot see you. The noise he is making is an expression of the anxiety he feels at being alone, so he needs to be taught that being alone is okay. You are not actually training the dog to stop making noise, you are training him to feel comfortable when he is alone and thus removing the need for him to make the noise. This is where the crate with cozy bedding and a favorite toy comes in handy. You want to know that he is safe when you are not there to supervise, and you know that he will be safe in his crate rather than roaming freely about the house. In order for the pup to stay in his crate without making a fuss, he needs to be comfortable in his crate. On that note, it is extremely important that the crate is never used as a form of punishment, or the pup

will develop a negative association with the crate.

Accustom the pup to the crate in short, gradually increasing time intervals in which you put him in the crate, maybe with a treat, and stay in the room with him. If he cries or makes a fuss, do not go to him, but stay in his sight. Gradually he will realize that staying in his crate is okay without your help, and it will not be so traumatic for him when you are not around. You may want to leave the radio on softly when you leave the house; the sound of human voices may be comforting to him.

Your wisest investment will be your Shih Tzu's crate. Introduce the puppy to the crate in small intervals, gradually increasing the amount of time he's expected to stay.

PUPPY PROBLEMS

The majority of problems that are commonly seen in young pups will disappear as your dog gets older. However, how you deal with problems when he is young will determine how he reacts to discipline as an adult dog. It is important to establish who is boss (hopefully it will be you!) right away when you are first bonding with your dog. This bond will set the tone for the rest of your life together.

DIETARY AND FEEDING CONSIDERATIONS

Today the choices of food for your Shih Tzu are many and varied. There are simply dozens of brands of food in all sorts of flavors and textures, ranging from puppy diets to those for seniors. There are even hypoallergenic and low-calorie diets available. Because your Shih Tzu's food has a bearing on coat, health and temperament, it is essential that the most suitable diet is selected for a Shih Tzu of his age. It is fair to say, however, that even dedicated owners can be somewhat perplexed by the enormous range of foods available. Only understanding what is best for your dog will help you reach an informed decision.

Dog foods are produced in three basic types: dry, semi-moist

and canned. Dry foods are useful for the cost-conscious for overall they tend to be less expensive than semi-moist or canned. These contain the least fat and the most preservatives. In general, canned foods are made up of 60–70% water, while semi-moist ones often contain so much sugar that they are perhaps the least preferred by owners, even though their dogs seem to like them.

When selecting your dog's diet, three stages of development must be considered: the puppy stage, the adult stage and the senior stage.

STORING DOG FOOD

You must store your dry dog food carefully. Open packages of dog food quickly lose their vitamin value, usually within 90 days of being opened. Mold spores and vermin could also contaminate the food.

PUPPY STAGE

Puppies instinctively want to suck milk from their mother's teats and a normal puppy will exhibit this behavior from just a few moments following birth. If puppies do not attempt to suckle within the first half-hour or so, the breeder should encourage them to do so by placing each pup on a nipple, having selected ones with plenty of milk. This

FOOD PREFERENCE

Selecting the best dry dog food is difficult. There is no majority consensus among veterinary scientists as to the value of nutrient analyses (protein, fat, fiber, moisture, ash, cholesterol, minerals, etc.). All agree that feeding trials are what matter most, but you also have to consider the individual dog. The dog's weight, age and activity level, and what pleases his taste, all must be considered. It is probably best to take the advice of your veterinarian. Every dog's dietary requirements vary, even during the lifetime of a particular dog.

If your dog is fed a good dry food, he does not require supplements of meat or vegetables. Dogs do appreciate a little variety in their diets, so you may choose to stay with the same brand but vary the flavor. Alternatively, you may wish to add a little flavored stock to give a difference to the taste.

early milk supply is important in providing colostrum to protect the puppies during the first eight to ten weeks of their lives. Although a mother's milk is much better than any milk formula, despite there being some excellent ones available, if the puppies do not feed, the breeder has to feed them himself. For those with less experience, advice from a veterinarian is important so that not only the right quantity of milk is fed but also that of correct quality, fed at suitably frequent intervals, usually every two hours during the first few days of life.

Puppies should be allowed to nurse from their dam for about the first six weeks, although from the third or fourth week the breeder will begin to introduce small portions of suitable solid food. Most breeders like to introduce alternate milk and meat meals initially, building up to weaning time.

Puppy diets should be well balanced so that additional vitamins, minerals and other supplements are not necessary.

Milk is usually offered as part of the weaning process until the pup is fed solely on solid food.

ADULT DIETS

A dog is considered an adult when he has stopped growing, so in general the diet of a Shih Tzu can be changed to an adult one at about 18 months of age. Again you should rely upon your veterinarian, breeder or dietary specialist to recommend an acceptable maintenance diet. Major dog-food manufacturers specialize in this type of food, and it is just necessary for you to select the one best suited to your dog's needs. Active dogs may have different requirements than sedate dogs.

SENIOR DIETS

As dogs get older, their metabolism changes. The older dog usually exercises less, moves more slowly and sleeps more. This change in lifestyle and physiological performance requires a change in diet. Since these changes take place slowly, they might not be recognizable. What is easily recognizable is weight gain. By continuing to feed your dog an adult-maintenance diet when it is slowing down metabolically, your dog will gain weight. Obesity in an older dog compounds the health problems that already accompany old age.

By the time the puppies are seven or a maximum of eight weeks old, they should be fully weaned and fed solely on a proprietary puppy food. Selection of the most suitable, good-quality diet at this time is essential for a puppy's fastest growth rate is during the first year of life. Veterinarians are usually able to offer advice in this regard and, although the frequency of meals will be reduced over time, only when a young dog has reached the age of about 18 months should an adult diet be fed.

Puppy and junior diets should be well balanced for the needs of your dog, so that except in certain circumstances additional vitamins, minerals and proteins will not be required.

As your dog gets older, few of his organs function up to par. The kidneys slow down and the intestines become less efficient. These age-related factors are best handled with a change in diet and

Once your Shih Tzu is completely house-trained, water should be available to him at all times.

a change in feeding schedule to give smaller portions that are more easily digested.

There is no single best diet for every older dog. While many dogs do well on light or senior diets, other dogs do better on puppy diets or other special premium diets such as lamb and rice. Be sensitive to your senior Shih Tzu's diet and this will help control other problems that may arise with your old friend.

WATER

Just as your dog needs proper nutrition from his food, water is

GRAIN-BASED DIETS

Some less expensive dog foods are based on grains and other plant proteins. While these products may appear to be attractively priced, many breeders prefer a diet based on animal proteins and believe that they are more conducive to your dog's health. Many grain-based diets rely on soy protein, which may cause flatulence (passing gas).

There are many cases, however, when your dog might require a special diet. These special requirements should only be recommended by your veterinarian.

The best exercise for any Shih Tzu is another Shih Tzu. This young puppy is following his adult pal around the yard in a game of tag!

an essential "nutrient" as well. Water keeps the dog's body properly hydrated and promotes normal function of the body's systems. During housebreaking, it is necessary to keep an eye on how much water your Shih Tzu is drinking, but once he is reliably trained he should have access to clean fresh water at all times. Make sure that the dog's water bowl is clean, and change the water often, making sure that water is always available for your dog, especially if you feed dry food.

EXERCISE

Although a Shih Tzu is small, all dogs require some form of exercise, regardless of breed. A sedentary lifestyle is as harmful to a dog as it is to a person. The Shih Tzu is a fairly active breed that enjoys exercise, but you don't have to be an Olympic athlete! Regular walks, play sessions in the yard, or letting the dog run free in a fenced enclosure under

your supervision are sufficient forms of exercise for the Shih Tzu. For those who are more ambitious, you will find that your Shih Tzu also enjoys longer walks or perhaps an occasional hike. Bear in mind that an overweight dog should never be suddenly over-exercised; instead he should be allowed to increase exercise slowly. Not only is exercise essential to keep the dog's body fit, it is also essential to his mental well-being. A bored dog will find something to do, which often manifests itself in some type of destructive behavior. In this sense, it is essential for the owner's mental well-being as well!

GROOMING

Your Shih Tzu will need to be groomed regularly, so it is essential that short grooming sessions are introduced from a very early age. From the very beginning, a few minutes each day should be set aside for grooming. Increase the duration of the sessions, building up slowly as the puppy matures and the coat grows in length. Your puppy should be taught to stand on a solid surface for grooming; a suitable table is one on which the dog will not slip. Under no circumstances should you leave your Shih Tzu alone on a table, for he may all too easily jump off and injure himself. Commercial grooming tables equipped with an overhead

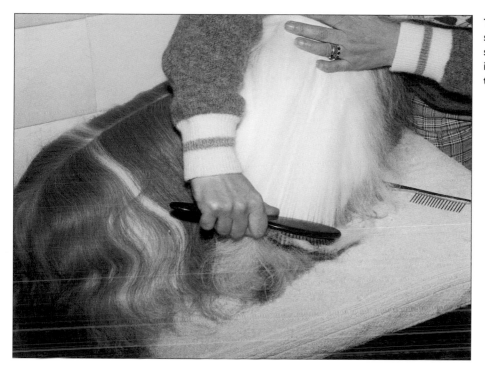

The Shih Tzu should be brushed, section by section, in the direction of the hair growth.

arm and holding "noose" are available at pet shops.

When the puppy is used to standing on the table, you will need to teach him to be rolled over onto his side. Do this by grasping his front and back legs on the opposite side of your own body, then gently placing him down by leaning over him for reassurance. To begin, just stroke his tummy so that he looks upon this new routine as something highly pleasurable. Then, when you know he is comfortable with this, introduce a few gentle brush strokes. Be sure you don't tug at any knots at this stage, for this would cause him to associate this routine with pain. It may take a little getting used to both for you and your puppy, but only if your Shih Tzu learns to lie down on his side will you easily be able to groom in all the awkward places. You will both be glad you had a little patience to learn this trick from the very start!

You will notice that not only does your Shih Tzu's coat grow longer with age but also, usually between 10 and 12 months of age, the coat changes from a puppy coat to an adult one. This can be a difficult time, for knots can form very easily and you will realize how comparatively easy grooming your youngster was!

69

Your local pet shop will have a variety of grooming tools, brushes and combs which will assist you in keeping your Shih Tzu's coat in peak condition.

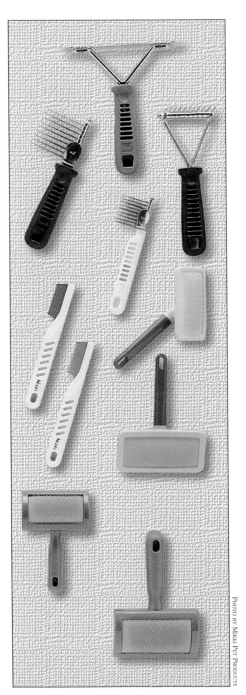

Photo by Mikki Pet Products

You will certainly need to groom the coat between bath times, but never groom the coat when completely dry. To avoid breaking the ends, use a light conditioning spray. Even water dispensed from a fine-spray bottle is better than no moisture at all.

ROUTINE GROOMING

With your Shih Tzu lying on his side, the coat should be parted, layered and brushed section by section, always in the direction of the coat growth. It is imperative to groom right down to the skin so that the undercoat is not left matted. After using a good-quality bristle brush, a wide-toothed comb can be used to finish each section.

GROOMING SUPPLIES

How much grooming equipment you purchase will depend on how much grooming you are going to do. Here are some basics:

- Natural bristle brush
- Metal comb
- Blow dryer
- Rubber mat
- Dog shampoo
- Spray hose attachment
- Ear cleaner
- Cotton balls
- Towels
- Scissors
- Conditioning spray
- Elastics for topknot
- Nail clippers

If you do find mats in your Shih Tzu's coat, spray the mat with a generous amount of conditioning or anti-tangle spray. Leave this to soak in for a few moments, then gently tease out the mat with your fingers. Always work from the inside out, or the knot will just get tighter! Tight knots will probably need to be teased out using a wide-toothed comb, but be careful not to tug at the knot. It will be painful for the pup, and will also pull out too much coat.

Take care in grooming the tummy and under the "armpits," for these areas are especially sensitive. There is really no harm in cutting away small tight knots from under the armpits, as these will not show and the dog will feel more comfortable. However, a Shih Tzu in show coat should not be trimmed, so scissors should only be used when absolutely necessary. Trimming below the pads of the feet prevents uncomfortable hairballs from forming between the pads. On males, most owners also trim off a little hair from the end of the penis, but a good half inch must be left so that tiny hairs do not aggravate the penis and set up infection. Whatever you do, take care not to cut through a nipple—and remember that males have little nipples too!

The legs and "pants" of a Shih Tzu are very heavily coated and will also need regular grooming.

To prevent knots and tangles, be sure to immediately remove any debris that may have accumulated following a visit outdoors. Also always check your dog's back end to see that nothing remains attached to the coat from his relief visits. Between baths you may like to use a damp sponge, but always be sure to dry the coat thoroughly. Drying will keep your Shih Tzu comfortable and will prevent the coat from curling too much.

Some Shih Tzu don't seem to mind having their feet groomed, while others hate it. Nonetheless, you will have to check the feet thoroughly on a regular basis. Be sure you don't allow knots to

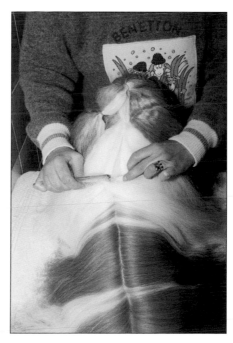

A wide-toothed comb can be used after the coat has been brushed.

71

The topknot on a Shih Tzu crowns the dog's glorious coat. Your breeder or a professional groomer can offer you some pointers on creating the perfect topknot.

build up between the toes, and always keep an eye on the length of the toenails.

HEAD, TOPKNOT AND FINISHING TOUCHES

It is essential to keep the whiskers, beard and eyes of a Shih Tzu clean, so these must be checked every day. Eyes can be cleaned with a canine liquid eye cleaner. The beard and whiskers can be washed and combed through, and some owners find it useful to attach elastic on each side of the beard to prevent soiling, especially when the dog is eating.

When grooming, pay special attention to the hair behind the ears. This hair is often of a finer texture and knots easily. From about five months of age, your Shih Tzu will have enough head hair to tie into a topknot. Comb up the hair from the stop, and fix it into a tiny elastic band. Most owners use dental elastics. Take care not to pull up the hair too tightly so that it pulls on the eyes. Elastics will generally need to be changed at least once a day. Never pull them out; instead, always cut them carefully with scissors so as not to damage any hair. Under no circumstances should the head hair of a Shih Tzu be trimmed for the show ring, although if a Shih Tzu is maintained in a pet trim the head hair can be cut short to match the rest of the coat. Some pet owners, though, like to keep long fringing on the ears.

When grooming is complete, use a wide-toothed comb to create a straight parting down the length of the back, so that the coat falls evenly on either side.

Bathing and Drying

How frequently you decide to bathe your Shih Tzu will depend very much on whether your dog is a show dog or a pet. Show dogs are usually bathed before every show, which may be as frequent as once a week. Pet dogs are usually bathed less frequently, especially if they are kept in puppy trim because the coat does not drag on the ground to pick up dirt and debris.

Every owner has his own preference as to how best to bathe, but ideally the coat should be groomed through before bathing. I like to stand my own dogs on a non-slip mat in the bath, then wet the coat thoroughly using a shower attachment. It is imperative that the water temperature is tested on your own hand before

spraying the dog. Use a good-quality shampoo designed especially for dogs, always stroking it into the coat rather than rubbing, so as not to create knots. When the shampoo has been thoroughly rinsed out, apply a canine condi-

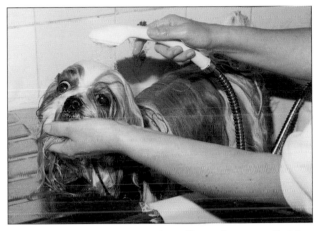

After shampooing, the dog should be thoroughly rinsed to remove all of the soap from the his coat.

After the dog has been thoroughly rinsed, wrap him in an absorbent bath towel and help him out of the tub. Once you release him, he'll shake the water from his coat, so be prepared!

Left: Use a blow dryer to dry his coat as thoroughly as possible. Never let your Shih Tzu dry naturally!

Right: Don't forget to do the belly region. Lay the dog on his back in your lap and use a blow dryer at very low heat.

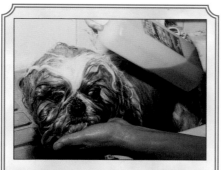

SOAP IT UP

The use of human soap products like shampoo, bubble bath and hand soap can be damaging to a dog's coat and skin. Use only shampoo made especially for dogs. You may like to use a medicated shampoo, which will help to keep external parasites at bay.

tioner in the same manner, then rinse again until the water runs clear. Many people like to use a baby shampoo on the head to avoid irritation to the eyes, and some like to plug the ears with cotton balls to avoid water getting inside them. Personally, I use neither of these. By just taking special care in those areas, I have never encountered problems.

Before taking your dog out of the bath, it is a good idea to use a highly absorbent cloth to soak up excess moisture. You can then lift your Shih Tzu out of the bath, wrapped in a clean towel. Undoubtedly your dog will want to shake—so be prepared!

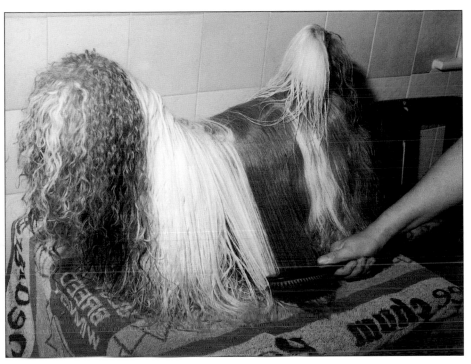

Use the brush to detangle and straighten the coat as you dry.

Drying can be done on the same table you use for the grooming process. Work systematically, all the while brushing as well as applying warm air from the hairdryer. Never just blow-dry the dog with the intention of grooming later, or your Shih Tzu's coat will not end up in good condition. Certainly you should never allow a Shih Tzu to dry naturally.

Put the finishing touches to your dog's coat, just as you would have done if grooming without a bath. Bathing and grooming a long-coated breed is always a lengthy task, but I assure you the end result will have made it all worthwhile.

BATHING BEAUTY

Once you are sure that the dog is thoroughly rinsed, squeeze the excess water out of his coat with your hand and dry him initially with a heavy towel. You will finish the drying job with a blow dryer on a low setting. In cold weather, never allow your dog outside with a wet coat.

There are "dry bath" products on the market, which are sprays and powders intended for spot cleaning, that can be used between regular baths if necessary. They are not substitutes for regular baths, but they are easy to use for touch-ups as they do not require rinsing.

This Shih Tzu has been put down in oil. After the bath, some groomers apply a mineral, vegetable or baby oil to the coat, working it from the roots to the ends of the hairs. This treatment to improve the coat is followed by hot towels or the blow dryer. Of course, the oil must be washed out after several minutes.

EAR CLEANING

Because the Shih Tzu has such a long coat, long hair will also grow inside the ears. This should be carefully plucked out either with special blunt-ended tweezers or, if you prefer, with your fingertips. If you always remove only a few hairs at a time, this should be entirely painless.

Ears should be kept clean. Ears can be cleaned with a cotton ball and special cleaner or ear powder made especially for dogs. Be on the lookout for any signs of infection or ear-mite infestation. If your Shih Tzu has been shaking his head or scratching at his ears frequently, this usually indicates a problem. If his ears have an unusual odor, this is a sure sign of mite infestation or infection, and a signal to have his ears checked by the veterinarian.

NAIL CLIPPING

Your Shih Tzu should be accustomed to having his nails trimmed at an early age, since it will be part of your maintenance routine throughout his life. Long nails can all too easily get caught in the Shih Tzu's long coat and can scratch someone unintentionally. Also, a long nail has a better chance of ripping and bleeding, or causing the feet to spread. A good rule of thumb is that if you can hear your dog's nails' clicking on the floor when he walks, his nails are too long.

Before you start cutting, make sure you can identify the "quick" in each nail. The quick is a blood vessel that runs through the center of each nail and grows rather close to the end. It will

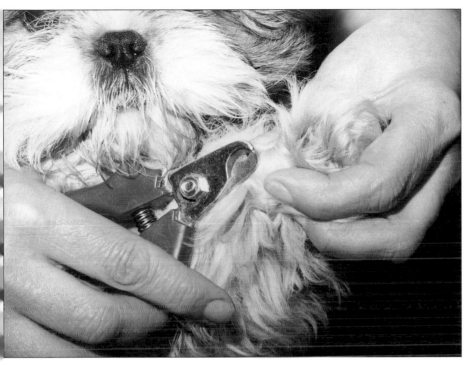

The nails should be carefully clipped with special dog nail clippers. Accustom your Shih Tzu to this from puppyhood and you will have a more cooperative adult.

The excess hair in the ears should be carefully plucked with blunt-ended tweezers (or your fingertips).

bleed if accidentally cut, which will be quite painful for the dog as it contains nerve endings. Keep some type of clotting agent on hand, such as a styptic pencil or styptic powder (the type used for shaving). This will stop the bleeding quickly when applied to the end of the cut nail. Do not panic if this happens, just stop the bleeding and talk soothingly to your dog. Once he has calmed down, move on to the next nail. It is better to clip a little at a time, particularly with black-nailed dogs.

Hold your pup steady as you begin trimming his nails; you do

The hair growing on the bottom of the Shih Tzu's foot, around the pad, should be trimmed short.

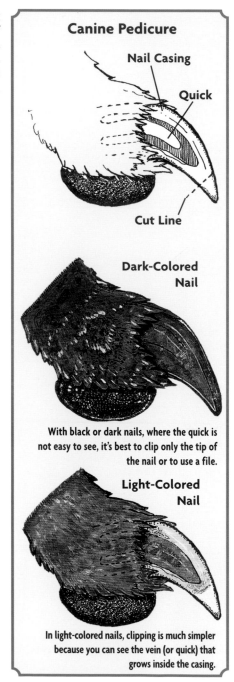

Canine Pedicure

Nail Casing

Quick

Cut Line

Dark-Colored Nail

With black or dark nails, where the quick is not easy to see, it's best to clip only the tip of the nail or to use a file.

Light-Colored Nail

In light-colored nails, clipping is much simpler because you can see the vein (or quick) that grows inside the casing.

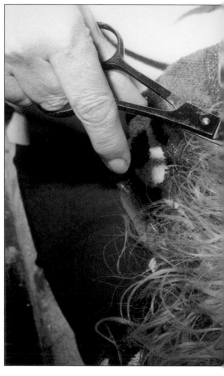

not want him to make any sudden movements or run away. Talk to him soothingly and stroke him as you clip. Holding his foot in your hand, simply take off the end of each nail in one quick clip. You can purchase nail clippers that are specially made for dogs; you can probably find them wherever you buy pet supplies.

TRAVELING WITH YOUR DOG
CAR TRAVEL
You should accustom your Shih Tzu to riding in a car at an early age. You may or may not take him in the car often, but at the very least he will need to go to the vet

The teeth of a puppy Shih Tzu.

The teeth of an adult Shih Tzu.

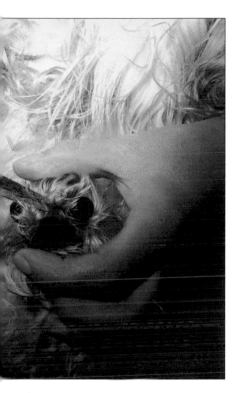

and you do not want these trips to be traumatic for the dog or a big hassle for you. The safest way for a dog to ride in the car is in his crate. If he uses a crate in the house, you can use the same crate for travel.

Put the pup in the crate and see how he reacts. If he seems uneasy, you can have a passenger hold him on his lap while you drive. Another option is a safety harness specially made for dogs, which straps the dog in much like a seat belt. Do not let the dog roam loose in the vehicle—this is very dangerous! If you should stop short, your dog can be

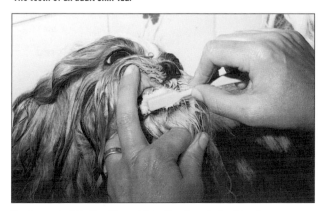

Brush your dog's teeth with special toothpaste and a toothbrush that are made for dogs.

thrown and injured. If the dog starts climbing on you and pestering you while you are driving, you will not be able to concentrate on the road. It is an unsafe situation for everyone—human and canine.

For long trips, be prepared to stop to let the dog relieve himself. Bring along whatever you need to clean up after him. You should take along some paper towels and perhaps some old bath towels for use should he have an accident in the car or suffer from motion sickness.

SHIH TZU IN THE FRIENDLY SKIES
Contact your chosen airline before proceeding with travel plans that include your Shih Tzu. The dog will be required to travel in a fiberglass crate and you should always check in advance with the airline regarding specific requirements for the crate's size, type and labeling. To help put the dog at ease, give him one of his favorite toys in the crate. Do not feed the

dog for several hours prior to checking in so that you minimize his need to relieve himself. Some airlines require you to provide documentation as to when the dog has last been fed. In any case, a light meal is best.

Make sure your dog is properly identified and that your contact information appears on his ID tags and on his crate.

When traveling with your Shih Tzu in a car, keep him in his crate. This is the safest, most acceptable way of traveling with a dog.

> **ON THE ROAD**
> If you are going on a long road trip with your dog, be sure the hotels are dog-friendly. Many hotels do not accept dogs. Also take along some ice that can be thawed and offered to your dog if he becomes overheated. Most dogs like to lick ice.

Although most dogs travel in a different area of the plane than the human passengers, the Shih Tzu is fortunate enough to travel in "coach" (or "first-class") along with his owners! Most airlines provide for toy dogs to travel with their owners, and Shih Tzu owners should always seek out airlines willing to accommodate their dogs first!

Crate training pays off when your Shih Tzu has to travel in his crate. He will not feel confined and uncomfortable, but rather feel quite "at home" for the trip.

VACATIONS AND BOARDING

So you want to take a family vacation—and you want to include *all* members of the family. You would probably make arrangements for accommodations ahead of time anyway, but this is especially

GOING ABROAD

For international travel, you will have to make arrangements well in advance (perhaps months), as countries' regulations pertaining to bringing in animals differ. There may be special health certificates and/or vaccinations that your dog will need before taking the trip; sometimes this has to be done within a certain time frame. When traveling to rabies-free countries, you will need to bring proof of the dog's rabies vaccination and there will likely be a quarantine period upon arrival.

important when traveling with a dog. You do not want to make an overnight stop at the only place around for miles and find out that they do not allow dogs. Also, you do not want to reserve a place for your family without confirming that you are traveling with a dog because if it is against their policy you may not have a place to stay.

Alternatively, if you are traveling and choose not to bring your Shih Tzu, you will have to make arrangements for him while you are away. Some options are to take him to a neighbor's house to stay while you are gone, to have a trusted neighbor stop by often or stay at your house or to bring your dog to a reputable boarding kennel. If you choose to board him at a kennel, you should visit in advance to see the facility, how clean it is and where the dogs are kept. Talk to some of the employees and see how they treat the dogs—have they experience in grooming long-coated dogs, do they spend time with the dogs,

play with them, exercise them, etc.? Also find out the kennel's policy on vaccinations and what they require. This is for all of the dogs' safety, since when dogs are kept together, there is a greater risk of diseases being passed from dog to dog.

IDENTIFICATION
Your Shih Tzu is your valued companion and friend. That is why you always keep a close eye on him and you have made sure that he cannot escape from the yard or wriggle out of his collar and run away from you. However, accidents can happen and there may come a time when your dog unexpectedly gets separated from you. If this unfortunate event

TRAVEL TIP
The most extensive travel you do with your dog may be limited to trips to the veterinarian's office—or you may decide to bring him along for long distances when the family goes on vacation. Whichever the case, it is important to consider your dog's safety while traveling.

should occur, the first thing on your mind will be finding him. Proper identification, including an ID tag and possibly a tattoo and/or a microchip, will increase the chances of his being returned to you safely and quickly.

PERMANENT ID

As puppies become more and more expensive, especially those puppies of high quality for showing and/or breeding, they have a greater chance of being stolen. The usual collar dog tag is, of course, easily removed. But there are two permanent techniques that have become widely utilized for identification.

The puppy microchip implantation involves the injection of a small microchip, about the size of a corn kernel, under the skin of the dog. If your dog shows up at a clinic or shelter, or is offered for resale under less than savory circumstances, he can be positively identified by the microchip. The microchip is scanned and a registry quickly identifies you as the owner. This is more than protection against theft, but should the dog run away or go chasing a squirrel and get lost, you have a fair chance of getting him back.

Tattooing is done on various parts of the dog, from his belly to his cheeks. The number tattooed can be your telephone number or his AKC registration number. When professional dog thieves see a tattooed dog, they usually lose interest. For the safety of our dogs, no laboratory facility or dog broker will accept a tattooed dog as stock. Both microchipping and tattooing can be done at your local veterinary clinic.

Proper identification tags are a simple way to ensure that you will be able to retrieve your dog should he wander away from home.

Living with an untrained dog is a lot like owning a piano that you do not know how to play—it is a nice object to look at but it does not do much more than that to bring you pleasure. Now try taking piano lessons and suddenly the piano comes alive and brings forth magical sounds and rhythms that set your heart singing and your body swaying.

The same is true with your Shih Tzu. Any dog is a big responsibility and if not trained sensibly may develop unacceptable behavior that annoys you or could even cause family friction.

REAP THE REWARDS

If you start with a normal, healthy dog and give him time, patience and some carefully executed lessons, you will reap the rewards of that training for the life of the dog. And what a life it will be! The two of you will find immeasurable pleasure in the companionship you have built together with love, respect and understanding.

To train your Shih Tzu, you may like to enroll in an obedience class. Teach him good manners as you learn how and why he behaves the way he does. Find out how to communicate with your dog and how to recognize and understand his communications with you. Suddenly the dog takes on a new role in your life—he is smart, interesting, well behaved and fun to be with. He demonstrates his bond of devotion to you daily. In other words, your Shih Tzu does wonders for your ego because he constantly reminds you that you are not only his leader, you are his hero!

Those involved with teaching dog obedience and counseling owners about their dogs' behavior have discovered some interesting facts about dog ownership. For example, training dogs when they are puppies results in the highest rate of success in developing well-mannered and well-adjusted adult dogs. Training an older dog, from six months to six years of age, can produce almost equal results providing that the owner accepts the dog's slower rate of learning capability and is willing to work patiently to help the dog succeed at developing to his fullest potential. Unfortunately, many owners of untrained adult dogs lack the patience factor, so they do not persist until their dogs are successful at learning particular behaviors.

Training a puppy aged 10 to 16 weeks (20 weeks at the most) is like working with a dry sponge in a pool of water. The pup soaks up whatever you show him and constantly looks for more things to do and learn. At this early age, his body is not yet producing hormones, and therein lies the reason for such a high rate of success. Without hormones, he is focused on his owners and not particularly interested in investigating other places, dogs, people, etc. You are his leader: his provider of food, water, shelter and security. He latches onto you and wants to stay close. He will usually follow you from room to room, will not let you out of his sight when you are outdoors with him, and respond in like manner to the people and animals you encounter. If you greet a friend warmly, he will be happy to greet the person as well. If, however, you are hesitant, even anxious, about the approach of a stranger, he will respond accordingly.

Once the puppy begins to produce hormones, his natural curiosity emerges and he begins to investigate the world around him. It is at this time when you may notice that the untrained dog begins to wander away from you and even ignore your commands to stay close.

There are usually classes within a reasonable distance of the owner's home, but you can also do a lot to train your dog yourself. Sometimes there are classes available but the tuition is too costly. Whatever the circumstances, the solution to the prob-

PARENTAL GUIDANCE
Training a dog is a life experience. Many parents admit that much of what they know about raising children they learned from caring for their dogs. Dogs respond to love, fairness and guidance, just as children do. Become a good dog owner and you may become an even better parent.

Male dogs have a strong desire to mark their territory. Females generally are easier to housebreak than males, since males tend to worry more about where to relieve themselves.

lem of training your Shih Tzu without formal obedience lessons lies within the pages of this book.

This chapter is devoted to helping you train your Shih Tzu at home. If the recommended procedures are followed faithfully, you may expect positive results that will prove rewarding to both you and your dog.

Whether your new charge is a puppy or a mature adult, the methods of teaching and the techniques we use in training basic behaviors are the same. After all, no dog, whether puppy or adult,

likes harsh or inhumane methods. All creatures, however, respond favorably to gentle motivational methods and sincere praise and encouragement. Now let us get started.

HOUSEBREAKING
You can train a puppy to relieve himself wherever you choose, but this must be somewhere suitable. You should bear in mind from the outset that when your puppy is old enough to go out in public places, any canine deposits must be removed at once. You will always have to carry with you a small plastic bag or "poop-scoop."

Outdoor training includes such surfaces as grass, dirt and cement. Indoor training usually means training your dog to newspaper. When deciding on the surface and location that you will want your Shih Tzu to use, be sure it is going to be permanent. Training your dog to grass and then changing your mind two months later is extremely difficult for both dog and owner.

Next, choose the command you will use each and every time you want your puppy to void. "Go hurry up" and "Potty time" are examples of commands commonly used by dog owners. Get in the habit of giving the puppy your chosen relief command before you take him out. That way, when he becomes

THINK BEFORE YOU BARK
Dogs are sensitive to their masters' moods and emotions. Use your voice wisely when communicating with your dog. Never raise your voice at your dog unless you are angry and trying to correct him. "Barking" at your dog can become as meaningless as "dogspeak" is to you.

an adult, you will be able to determine if he wants to go out when you ask him. A confirmation will be signs of interest such as wagging his tail, watching you intently, going to the door, etc.

PUPPY'S NEEDS

The puppy needs to relieve himself after play periods, after each meal, after he has been sleeping and any time he indicates that he is looking for a place to urinate or defecate. The urinary and intestinal tract muscles of very young puppies are not fully developed. Therefore, like human babies, puppies need to relieve themselves frequently.

Take your puppy out often—every hour for an eight-week-old, for example, and always immediately after sleeping and eating. The older the puppy, the less often he will need to relieve himself. Finally, as a mature healthy adult, he will require only three to five relief trips per day.

HOUSING

Since the types of housing and control you provide for your puppy have a direct relationship on the success of house-training, we consider the various aspects of both before we begin training. Bringing a new puppy home and turning him loose in your house can be compared to turning a child loose in a sports arena and telling the child that the place is

PAPER CAPER
Never line your pup's sleeping area with newspaper. Puppy litters are usually raised on newspaper and, once in your home, the puppy will immediately associate newspaper with voiding. Never leave newspaper on any floor while house-training, as this will only confuse the puppy. If you are paper-training him, use paper in his designated relief area only. Finally, restrict water intake after evening meals. Offer a few licks at a time—never let a young puppy gulp water after meals.

all his! The sheer enormity of the place would be too much for him to handle.

Instead, offer the puppy clearly defined areas where he

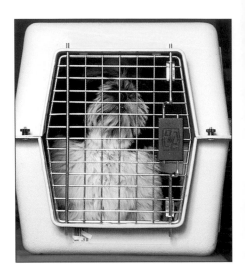

Dogs do not like to soil where they sleep. Let your puppy out often to relieve himself so he is not uncomfortable trying to "hold it" in his crate.

can play, sleep, eat and live. A room of the house where the family gathers is the most obvious choice. Puppies are social animals and need to feel a part of the pack right from the start. Hearing your voice, watching you while you are doing things and smelling you nearby are all positive reinforcers that he is now a member of your pack. Usually a family room, the kitchen or a nearby adjoining breakfast area is ideal for providing safety and security for both puppy and owner.

Within that room there should be a smaller area which the puppy can call his own. A wire or fiberglass dog crate from which he can view the activities of his new family will be ideal. The size of the crate is the key factor here. The area must be large enough for the puppy to lie down and stretch out as well as stand up without rubbing his head on the top, yet small enough so that he cannot relieve himself at one end and sleep at the other without coming into contact with his droppings before he is fully trained to relieve himself outside.

Dogs are, by nature, clean animals and will not remain close to their relief areas unless forced to do so. In those cases, they then become dirty dogs and usually remain that way for life.

The designated area should be lined with clean bedding and a toy. Once he is reliably house-trained, water can be available, in a non-spill container.

CONTROL

By *control*, we mean helping the puppy to create a lifestyle pattern that will be compatible to that of his human pack (you!). Just as we guide little children to learn our way of life, we must show the

---

CALM DOWN

Dogs will do anything for your attention. If you reward the dog when he is calm and resting, you will develop a well-mannered dog. If, on the other hand, you greet your dog excitedly and encourage him to wrestle with you, the dog will greet you the same way and you will have a hyperactive dog on your hands.

Canine Development Schedule

It is important to understand how and at what age a puppy develops into adulthood. If you are a puppy owner, consult the following Canine Development Schedule to determine the stage of development your Shih Tzu puppy is currently experiencing. This knowledge will help you as you work with the puppy in the weeks and months ahead.

Period	Age	Characteristics
FIRST TO THIRD	BIRTH TO SEVEN WEEKS	Puppy needs food, sleep and warmth, and responds to simple and gentle touching. Needs mother for security and disciplining. Needs littermates for learning and interacting with other dogs. Pup learns to function within a pack and learns pack order of dominance. Begin socializing with adults and children for short periods. Begins to become aware of his environment.
FOURTH	EIGHT TO TWELVE WEEKS	Brain is fully developed. Needs socializing with outside world. Remove from mother and littermates. Needs to change from canine pack to human pack. Human dominance necessary. Fear period occurs between 8 and 16 weeks. Avoid fright and pain.
FIFTH	THIRTEEN TO SIXTEEN WEEKS	Training and formal obedience should begin. Less association with other dogs, more with people, places, situations. Period will pass easily if you remember this is pup's change-to-adolescence time. Be firm and fair. Flight instinct prominent. Permissiveness and over-disciplining can do permanent damage. Praise for good behavior.
JUVENILE	FOUR TO EIGHT MONTHS	Another fear period about 7 to 8 months of age. It passes quickly, but be cautious of fright and pain. Sexual maturity reached. Dominant traits established. Dog should understand sit, down, come and stay by now.

NOTE: THESE ARE APPROXIMATE TIME FRAMES. ALLOW FOR INDIVIDUAL DIFFERENCES IN PUPPIES.

puppy when it is time to play, eat, sleep, exercise and even entertain himself.

Your puppy should always sleep in his crate. He should also learn that, during times of household confusion and excessive human activity such as at breakfast when family members are preparing for the day, he can play by himself in relative safety and comfort in his designated area. Each time you leave the puppy alone, he should understand

An open crate is fine for inside your home. For puppies, however, never put the water bowl inside the crate. This invites accidents when the puppy is crated.

exactly where he is to stay. You can gradually increase the time he is left alone to get him used to it. Puppies are chewers. They cannot tell the difference between safe chew toys and lamp cords, television wires, shoes, table legs, etc. Chewing into a television wire, for example, can be fatal to the puppy while a shorted wire can start a fire in the house.

If the puppy chews the arm of the chair when he is alone, you will probably discipline him angrily when you get home. Thus, he makes the association

> **TAKE THE LEAD**
> Do not carry your dog to his relief area. Lead him there on a leash or, better yet, encourage him to follow you to the spot. If you start carrying him to his spot, you might end up doing this routine forever and your dog will have the satisfaction of having trained *you*.

that your coming home means he is going to be punished. (He will not remember chewing up the chair and is incapable of making the association of the discipline with his naughty deed.)

Other times of excitement, such as family parties, visits, etc., can be fun for the puppy providing he can view the activities from the security of his designated area. He is not underfoot and he is not being fed all sorts of tidbits that will probably cause him stomach distress, yet he still feels a part of the fun.

SCHEDULE

A puppy should be taken to his relief area each time he is released from his designated area, after meals, after a play session, when he first awakens in the morning (at age eight weeks, this can mean 5 a.m.!). The puppy will indicate that he's ready "to go" by circling or sniffing busily—do not misinterpret these signs. For a puppy less than ten weeks of age, a routine of taking him out every hour is necessary. As the puppy grows, he will be able to wait for longer periods of time.

Keep trips to his relief area short. Stay no more than five or six minutes and then return to the house. If he goes during that time, praise him lavishly and take him indoors immediately. If he does not, but he has an accident when you go back indoors, pick him up immediately, say "No! No!" and return to his relief area. Wait a few minutes, then return to the house again. Never hit a puppy or put his face in urine or excrement when he has an accident!

Once indoors, put the puppy in his crate until you have had time to clean up his accident. Then release him to the family area and watch him more closely than before. Chances are, his accident was a result of your not picking up his signal or waiting too long before offering him the opportunity to relieve himself. Never hold a grudge against the puppy for accidents.

Let the puppy learn that going outdoors means it is time to relieve himself, not play. Once trained, he will be able to play indoors and out and still differentiate between the times for play versus the times for relief.

Help him develop regular hours for naps, being alone, playing by himself and just resting, all in

his crate. Encourage him to entertain himself while you are busy with your activities. Let him learn that having you near is comforting, but it is not your main purpose in life to provide him with undivided attention.

Each time you put your puppy in his own area, use the same

THE GOLDEN RULE
The golden rule of dog training is simple. For each "question" (command), there is only one correct answer (reaction). One command = one reaction. Keep practicing the command until the dog reacts correctly without hesitating. Be repetitive but not monotonous. Dogs get bored just as people do!

command, whatever suits best. Soon, he will run to his crate or special area when he hears you say those words.

Crate training provides safety for you, the puppy and the home. It also provides the puppy with a feeling of security, and that helps the puppy achieve self-confidence and clean habits.

Remember that one of the primary ingredients in house-training your puppy is control.

THE SUCCESS METHOD
6 Steps to Successful Crate Training

Success that comes by luck is usually short-lived. Success that comes by well-thought-out proven methods is often more easily achieved and permanent. This is the Success Method. It is designed to give you, the puppy owner, a simple yet proven way to help your puppy develop clean living habits and a feeling of security in his new environment.

1 Tell the puppy "Crate time!" and place him in the crate with a small treat (a piece of cheese or half of a biscuit). Let him stay in the crate for five minutes while you are in the same room. Then release him and praise lavishly. Never release him when he is fussing. Wait until he is quiet before you let him out.

2 Repeat Step 1 several times a day.

3 The next day, place the puppy in the crate as before. Let him stay there for ten minutes. Do this several times.

4 Continue building time in five-minute increments until the puppy stays in his crate for 30 minutes with you in the room. Always take him to his relief area after prolonged periods in his crate.

5 Now go back to Step 1 and let the puppy stay in his crate for five minutes, this time while you are out of the room.

6 Once again, build crate time in five-minute increments with you out of the room. When the puppy will stay willingly in his crate (he may even fall asleep!) for 30 minutes with you out of the room, he will be ready to stay in it for several hours at a time.

HOW MANY TIMES A DAY?

AGE	RELIEF TRIPS
To 14 weeks	10
14–22 weeks	8
22–32 weeks	6
Adulthood	4
(dog stops growing)	

These are estimates, of course, but they are a guide to the *minimum* number of opportunities a dog should have each day to relieve himself.

Always clean up after your dog, whether you're in a public place or your own yard.

Regardless of your lifestyle, there will always be occasions when you will need to have a place where your dog can stay and be happy and safe. Training is the answer for now and in the future.

In conclusion, a few key elements are really all you need for a successful house-training method—consistency, frequency, praise, control and supervision. By following these procedures with a normal, healthy puppy, you and the puppy will soon be past the stage of accidents and ready to move on to a clean and rewarding life together.

ROLES OF DISCIPLINE, REWARD AND PUNISHMENT

Discipline, training one to act in accordance with rules, brings order to life. It is as simple as that. Without discipline, particularly in a group society, chaos reigns supreme and the group will eventually perish. Humans and canines are social animals and need some form of discipline in order to function effectively. They must procure food, reproduce to keep the species going and protect their home base and their young. If there were no discipline in the lives of social animals, they would eventually die from starvation and/or predation by other stronger animals. In the case of domestic canines, dogs need

Your Shih Tzu will learn to regard his crate as his clean, quiet place of his own.

93

their satisfaction with their relationships with their dogs. People who had trained their dogs were 75% more satisfied with their pets than those who had never trained their dogs.

Dr. Edward Thorndike, a noted psychologist, established *Thorndike's Theory of Learning*, which states that a behavior that results in a pleasant event tends to be repeated. Likewise, a behavior that results in an unpleasant event tends not to be repeated. It is this theory on which training methods are based today. For example, if you manipulate a dog to perform a specific behavior and reward him for doing it, he is likely to do it again because he enjoyed the end result.

Occasionally, punishment, a penalty inflicted for an offense, is necessary. The best type of punishment often comes from an outside source. For example, a child is told not to touch the stove because he may get burned. He disobeys and touches the stove. In doing so, he receives a burn. From that time on, he respects the heat of the stove and avoids contact with it. Therefore, a behavior that results in an unpleasant event tends not to be repeated.

A good example of a dog learning the hard way is the dog who chases the house cat. He is told many times to leave the cat alone, yet he persists in teasing the cat. Then, one day he begins

When performing brings forth happy rewards, the Shih Tzu will readily repeat the behavior. Shih Tzu can be trained to do almost anything!

discipline in their lives in order to understand how their pack (you and other family members) functions and how they must act in order to survive.

A large humane society in a highly populated area recently surveyed dog owners regarding

PLAN TO PLAY

The puppy should also have regular play and exercise sessions when he is with you or a family member. Exercise for a very young puppy can consist of a short walk around the house or yard. Playing can include fetching games with a large ball or a special toy. (All puppies teethe and need soft things upon which to chew.) Remember to restrict play periods to indoors within his living area (the family room, for example) until he is completely house-trained.

chasing the cat but the cat turns and swipes a claw across the dog's face, leaving him with a painful gash on his nose. The final result is that the dog stops chasing the cat.

TRAINING EQUIPMENT
COLLAR AND LEAD
For a Shih Tzu the collar and lead that you use for training must be one with which you are easily able to work, not too heavy for the dog and perfectly safe.

TREATS
Have a bag of treats on hand. Something nutritious and easy to swallow works best. Use a soft treat, a chunk of cheese or a piece of cooked chicken rather than a dry biscuit. By the time the dog gets done chewing a dry treat, he will forget why he is being rewarded in the first place! As a sidebar, using food rewards will not teach a dog to beg at the table—the only way to teach a dog to beg at the table is to give him food from the table. In training, rewarding the dog with a food treat will help him associate praise and the treats with learning new behaviors that obviously please his owner.

TRAINING BEGINS:
ASK THE DOG A QUESTION
In order to teach your dog anything, you must first get his attention. After all, he cannot

LANGUAGE BARRIER
Dogs do not understand our language. They can be trained to react to a certain sound, at a certain volume. If you say "No, Oliver" in a very soft, pleasant voice, it will not have the same meaning as "No, Oliver!!" when you say it loudly. You should never use the dog's name during a reprimand, just the command "No!"

learn anything if he is looking away from you with his mind on something else.

To get his attention, ask him "School?" and immediately walk over to him and give him a treat as you tell him "Good dog." Wait a minute or two and repeat the routine, this time with a treat in your hand as you approach within a foot of the dog. Do not go directly to him, but stop about a foot short of him and hold out the treat as you ask "School?" He will see you approaching with a treat in your hand and most likely begin walking toward you. As you meet, give him the treat and praise again.

The third time, ask the question, have a treat in your hand and walk only a short distance toward the dog so that he must walk almost all the way to you.

Good performances during training should be rewarded with a treat. Treats really inspire dogs to perform.

As he reaches you, give him the treat and praise again.

By this time, the dog will probably be getting the idea that if he pays attention to you, especially when you ask that question, it will pay off in treats and fun activities for him. In other words, he learns that "school" means doing fun things with you that result in treats and positive attention for him.

Remember that the dog does not understand your verbal language, he only recognizes sounds. Your question translates to a series of sounds for him, and those sounds become the signal to go to you and pay attention; if he does, he will get to interact with you plus receive treats and praise.

THE BASIC COMMANDS
TEACHING SIT

Now that you have the dog's attention, attach his lead and hold it in your left hand and a food treat in your right. Place your food hand at the dog's nose and let him lick the treat but not take it from you. Say "Sit" and slowly raise your food hand from in front of the dog's nose up over his head so that he is looking at the ceiling. As he bends his head upward, he will have to bend his knees to maintain his balance. As he bends his knees, he will assume a sit position. At that point, release the food treat and praise lavishly with comments such as "Good dog! Good sit!" Remember to always praise enthusiastically, because dogs relish verbal praise from their owners and feel so proud of

TRAINING RULES

If you want to be successful in training your dog, you have four rules to obey yourself:
1. Develop an understanding of how a dog thinks.
2. Do not blame the dog for lack of communication.
3. Define your dog's personality and act accordingly.
4. Have patience and be consistent.

"Good dog! Good sit!" Teaching the sit is the beginning of your Shih Tzu's education.

themselves whenever they accomplish a behavior.

You will not use food forever in getting the dog to obey your commands. Food is only used to teach new behaviors, and once the dog knows what you want when

you give a specific command, you will wean him off the food treats but still maintain the verbal praise. After all, you will always have your voice with you, and there will be many times when you have no food rewards but expect the dog to obey.

It is better to use a soft treat, in small pieces, to reward your Shih Tzu. Cheese or a freeze-dried liver is an ideal treat.

TEACHING DOWN

Teaching the down exercise is easy when you understand how the dog perceives the down position, and it is very difficult when you do not. Dogs perceive the down position as a submissive one; therefore, teaching the down exercise using a forceful method can sometimes make the dog develop such a fear of the down that he either runs away when

DOUBLE JEOPARDY

A dog in jeopardy never lies down. He stays alert on his feet because instinct tells him that he may have to run away or fight for his survival. Therefore, if a dog feels threatened or anxious, he will not lie down. Consequently, it is important to keep the dog calm and relaxed as he learns the down exercise.

top of the dog's shoulders where they meet above the spinal cord. Do not push down on the dog's shoulders; simply rest your left hand there so you can guide the dog to lie down close to your left leg rather than to swing away from your side when he drops.

Now place the food hand at the dog's nose, say "Down" very softly (almost a whisper) and slowly lower the food hand to the dog's front feet. When the food hand reaches the floor, begin moving it forward along the floor in front of the dog. Keep talking softly to the dog, saying things like, "Do you want this treat? You can do this, good dog." Your reassuring tone of voice will help calm the dog as he tries to follow the food hand in order to get the treat.

When the dog's elbows touch the floor, release the food and praise softly. Try to get the dog to maintain that down position for several seconds before you let him sit up again. The goal here is to get the dog to settle down and not feel threatened in the down position.

TEACHING STAY

It is easy to teach the dog to stay in either a sit or a down position. Again, we use food and praise during the teaching process as we help the dog to understand exactly what it is that we are expecting him to do.

you say "Down" or he attempts to snap at the person who tries to force him down.

Have the dog sit close alongside your left leg, facing in the same direction as you are. Hold the lead in your left hand and a food treat in your right. Now place your left hand lightly on the

To teach the sit/stay, start with the dog sitting on your left side as before and hold the lead in your left hand. Have a food treat in your right hand and place your food hand at the dog's nose. Say "Stay" and step out on your right foot to stand directly in front of the dog, toe to toe, as he licks and nibbles the treat. Be sure to keep his head facing upward to maintain the sit position. Count to five and then swing around to stand next to the dog again with him on your left. As soon as you get back to the original position, release the food and praise lavishly.

To teach the down/stay, do the down as previously described. As soon as the dog lies down, say "Stay" and step out on your right foot just as you did in the sit/stay Count to five and then return to stand beside the dog with him on your left side. Release the treat and praise as always.

Within a week or ten days, you can begin to add a bit of

Teaching to stay begins either in the sitting or down position.

distance between you and your dog when you leave him. When you do, use your left hand open with the palm facing the dog as a stay signal, much the same as the hand signal a police officer uses to stop traffic at an intersection. Hold the food treat in your right hand as before, but this time the food is not touching the dog's nose. He will watch the food hand and quickly learn that he is going to get that treat as soon as you return to his side.

When you can stand 1 yard away from your dog for 30 seconds, you can then begin building time and distance in

You can use a treat to enhance your dog's desire to learn, but eventually the dog must be weaned off the food rewards.

Keeping your Shih Tzu's attention is half the lesson, especially with an intelligent, alert breed like this one.

Keeping your Shih Tzu's attention is half the lesson, especially with an intelligent, alert breed like this one.

both stays. Eventually, the dog can be expected to remain in the stay position for prolonged periods of time until you return to him or call him to you. Always praise lavishly when he stays.

TEACHING COME

If you make teaching "come" a fun experience, you should never have a student that does not love the game or that fails to come when called. The secret, it seems, is never to teach the word "come."

At times when an owner most wants his dog to come when called, the owner is likely upset

or anxious and he allows these feelings to come through in the tone of his voice when he calls his dog. Hearing that desperation

"WHERE ARE YOU?"

When calling the dog, do not say "Come." Say things like, "Rover, where are you? See if you can find me! I have a biscuit for you!" Keep up a constant line of chatter with coaxing sounds and frequent questions such as "Where are you?" The dog will learn to follow the sound of your voice to locate you and receive his reward.

in his owner's voice, the dog fears the results of going to him and therefore either disobeys outright or runs in the opposite direction. The secret, therefore, is to teach the dog a game and, when you want him to come to you, simply play the game. It is practically a no-fail solution!

To begin, have several members of your family take a few food treats and each go into a different room in the house. Take turns calling the dog, and each person should celebrate the dog's finding him with a treat and lots of happy praise. When a person calls the dog, he is actually inviting the dog to find him and get a treat as a reward for "winning."

A few turns of the "Where are you?" game and the dog will figure out that everyone is playing the game and that each person has a big celebration awaiting his success at locating him or her. Once he learns to love the game, simply calling out "Where are you?" will bring him running from wherever he is when he hears that all-important question.

The come command is recognized as one of the most important things to teach a dog, but there are trainers who work with thousands of dogs and never teach the actual word "come." Yet these dogs will race to respond to a person who uses the dog's name followed by "Where are you?" For example, a woman has a 12-year-

"COME" ... BACK
Never call your dog to come to you for a correction or scold him when he reaches you. That is the quickest way to turn a "Come" command into "Go away fast!" Dogs think only in the present tense, and your dog will connect the scolding with coming to you, not with the misbehavior of a few moments earlier.

old companion dog who went blind, but who never fails to locate her owner when asked, "Where are you?"

Children particularly love to play this game with their dogs. Children can hide in smaller places like a shower or bathtub, behind a bed or under a table. The dog needs to work a little bit harder to find these hiding places but when he does he loves to celebrate with a treat and a tussle with a favorite youngster.

TEACHING HEEL

Heeling means that the dog walks beside the owner without pulling. It takes time and patience on the owner's part to succeed at teaching the dog that he (the owner) will not proceed unless the dog is walking calmly beside him. Pulling out ahead on the lead is definitely not acceptable.

Begin with holding the lead in your left hand as the dog sits beside your left leg. Move the loop end of the lead to your right hand but keep your left hand short on the lead so it keeps the dog in close next to you.

FETCH!
Play fetch games with your puppy in an enclosed area where he can retrieve his toy and bring it back to you. Always use a toy or object designated just for this purpose. Never use a shoe, sock or other item he may later confuse with those in your closet or underneath your chair.

TUG OF WALK?
If you begin teaching the heel by taking long walks and letting the dog pull you along, he misinterprets this action as an acceptable form of taking a walk. When you pull back on the lead to counteract his pulling, he reads that tug as a signal to pull even harder!

Say "Heel" and step forward on your left foot. Keep the dog close to you and take three steps. Stop and have the dog sit next to you in what we now call the heel position. Praise verbally, but do not touch the dog. Hesitate a moment and begin again with "Heel," taking three steps and stopping, at which point the dog is told to sit again.

Your goal here is to have the dog walk those three steps without pulling on the lead. When he will walk calmly beside you for three steps without pulling, increase the number of steps you take to five. When he will walk politely beside you while you take five steps, you can increase the length of your walk to ten steps. Keep increasing the length of your stroll until the dog will walk quietly beside you without pulling as long as you want him to heel. When you stop heeling, indicate to the dog that the exercise is over by verbally praising as you pet him and say "OK, good dog." The "OK" is used

Each time the dog looks up at you or slows down to give a slack lead between the two of you, quietly praise him and say "Good heel. Good dog." Eventually, the dog will begin to respond and within a few days he will be walking politely beside you without pulling on the lead. At first, the training sessions should be kept short and very positive; soon the dog will be able to walk nicely with you for increasingly longer distances. Remember also to give the dog free time and the opportunity to run and play when you are done with heel practice.

Do not attempt to teach your dog more than one command in any given lesson. Keep training sessions short and sweet or you will lose your dog's attention.

WEANING OFF FOOD IN TREATS

Food is used in training new behaviors. Once the dog understands what behavior goes with a specific command, it is time to start weaning him off the food treats. At first, give a treat after each exercise. Then, start to give a treat only after every other exercise. Mix up the times when you offer a food reward and the times when you only offer praise so that the dog will never know when he is going to receive both food and praise and when he is going to receive only praise. This is called a variable ratio reward

as a release word, meaning that the exercise is finished and the dog is free to relax.

If you are dealing with a dog who insists on tugging on the lead, simply "put on your brakes" and stand your ground until the dog realizes that the two of you are not going anywhere until he is beside you and moving at your pace, not his. It may take some time just standing there to convince the dog that you are the leader and you will be the one to decide on the direction and speed of your travel.

Work diligently on the heel lesson and you will be rewarded with a dog who is a joy to walk his whole life.

This Shih Tzu is going through the pipe and collapsed tunnels at an agility trial.

> **FAMILY TIES**
> If you have other pets in the home and/or interact often with the pets of friends and other family members, your pup will respond to those pets in much the same manner as you do. It is only when you show fear of or resentment toward another animal that he will act fearful or unfriendly.

system and it proves successful because there is always the chance that the owner will produce a treat, so the dog never stops trying for that reward. No matter what, *always* give verbal praise.

OBEDIENCE AND OTHER ACTIVITIES
It is a good idea to enroll in an obedience class if one is available in your area. If yours is a show dog, handling classes would be more appropriate.

Many areas have dog clubs that offer basic obedience training as well as preparatory classes for obedience competition. There are also local dog trainers who offer similar classes.

At obedience trials, dogs can earn titles at various levels of competition. The beginning levels of competition include basic behaviors such as sit, down, heel, etc. The more

The well-trained Shih Tzu is a very focused competitor. He is very intelligent and can remember the obstacle course. What he lacks in leg, he makes up in brains.

advanced levels of competition include jumping, retrieving, scent discrimination and signal work. The advanced levels require a dog and owner to put a lot of time and effort into their training and the titles that can be earned at these levels of competition are very prestigious.

Teaching the dog to help out around the home, in the yard or on the farm provides great satisfaction to both dog and owner. In addition, the dog's help makes life a little easier for his owner and raises his stature as a valued companion to his family. It helps give the dog a purpose by occupying his mind and providing an outlet for his energy.

You can also consider trying your Shih Tzu's skill at an agility trial. Many dog clubs offer introductory courses in agility. Some Shih Tzu really enjoy the training and make enthusiastic and able competitors.

A BORN PRODIGY
Occasionally, a dog and owner who have not attended formal classes have been able to earn entry-level titles by obtaining competition rules and regulations from the hosting kennel club and practicing on their own to a degree of perfection. Obtaining the higher level agility and obedience titles, however, almost always requires extensive training under the tutelage of experienced instructors. In addition, the more difficult levels require more specialized equipment.

Shih Tzu are natural jumpers—whether it's the long jump or the high jump. Of course, agility trials adjust the size of the obstacles for the diminutive Shih Tzu.

The tunnel is no problem for this Shih Tzu, who zips through the obstacle at top speed.

Facing page: The Shih Tzu's innate intelligence and alert disposition qualify him for training many different arenas of the dog sport, from dog shows to tracking and agility.

Internal Structure of the Shih Tzu

1. Esophagus
2. Lungs
3. Gall Bladder
4. Liver
5. Kidney
6. Stomach
7. Intestines
8. Urinary Bladder

Dogs suffer from many of the same physical illnesses as people. They might even share many of the same psychological problems. Since people usually know more about human diseases than canine maladies, many of the terms used in this chapter will be familiar but not necessarily those used by veterinarians. We will use the term *x-ray*, instead of the more acceptable term *radiograph*. We will also use the familiar term *symptoms* even though dogs don't have symptoms, which are verbal descriptions of the patient's feelings, dogs have *clinical signs*. Since dogs can't speak, we have to look for clinical signs...but we still use the term *symptoms* in this book.

As a general rule, medicine is *practiced*. That term is not arbitrary. Medicine is a constantly changing art as we learn more and more about genetics, electronic aids (like CAT scans and MRIs) and daily laboratory advances.

There are many dog maladies, like canine hip dysplasia, which are not universally treated in the same manner. Some veterinarians opt for surgery more often than others do.

SELECTING A VETERINARIAN

Your selection of a veterinarian should be based not only upon his personality and skills with small dogs but also upon his convenience to your home. You want a vet who is close because you might have emergencies or need to make multiple visits for treatments. You want a vet who has services that you might require such as a boarding kennel and grooming facilities, as well as sophisticated pet supplies and a good reputation for ability and responsiveness. There is nothing more frustrating than having to wait a day or more to get a response from your veterinarian.

Before you buy your Shih Tzu, meet and interview the veterinarians in your area. Take everything into consideration; discuss background, specialties, fees, emergency policy, etc.

A typical vet's income, categorized according to services performed. This survey dealt with small-animal (pets) practices.

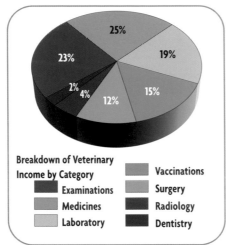

25%

19%

23%

2%
4%

15%

12%

Breakdown of Veterinary Income by Category

- Examinations
- Medicines
- Laboratory
- Vaccinations
- Surgery
- Radiology
- Dentistry

All veterinarians are licensed and their diplomas and/or certificates should be displayed in their waiting rooms. There are, however, many veterinary specialties that usually require further studies and internships. There are specialists in heart problems (veterinary cardiologists), skin problems (veterinary dermatologists), teeth and gum problems (veterinary dentists), eye problems (veterinary ophthalmologists) and x-rays (veterinary radiologists), and vets who have specialties in bones, muscles or certain organs. Most veterinarians do routine surgery such as neutering, stitching up wounds and docking tails for those breeds in which such is required for show purposes. When the problem affecting your dog is serious, it is not unusual or impudent to get another medical opinion, although it is courteous to advise the vets concerned about this. You might also want to compare costs among several veterinarians. Sophisticated health care and veterinary services can be very costly. Don't be bashful about discussing these costs with your veterinarian or his staff. It is not infrequent that important decisions are based upon financial considerations.

PREVENTATIVE MEDICINE
It is much easier, less costly and more effective to practice preventative medicine than to fight bouts of illness and disease. Properly bred puppies come from parents that were selected based upon their genetic-disease profiles. Their mother should have been vaccinated, free of all internal and external parasites and properly nourished. For these reasons, a visit to the veterinarian who cared for the dam is recommended. The dam

NEUTERING/SPAYING
Male dogs are castrated. The operation removes both testicles and requires that the dog be anesthetized. Recovery takes about one week. Females are spayed; in this operation, the uterus (womb) and both of the ovaries are removed. This is major surgery, also carried out under general anesthesia, and it usually takes a bitch two weeks to recover.

First Aid at a Glance

Burns
Place the affected area under cool water; use ice if only a small area is burnt.

Bee stings/Insect bites
Apply ice to relieve swelling; antihistamine dosed properly.

Animal bites
Clean any bleeding area; apply pressure until bleeding subsides; go to the vet.

Spider bites
Use cold compress and a pressurized pack to inhibit venom's spreading.

Antifreeze poisoning
Induce vomiting with hydrogen peroxide. Seek *immediate* veterinary help!

Fish hooks
Removal best handled by vet; hook must be cut in order to remove.

Snake bites
Pack ice around bite; contact vet quickly; identify snake for proper antivenin.

Car accident
Move dog from roadway with blanket; seek veterinary aid.

Shock
Calm the dog; keep him warm; seek immediate veterinary help.

Nosebleed
Apply cold compress to the nose; apply pressure to any visible abrasion.

Bleeding
Apply pressure above the area; treat wound by applying a cotton pack.

Heat stroke
Submerge dog in cold bath; cool down with fresh air and water; go to the vet.

Frostbite/Hypothermia
Warm the dog with a warm bath, electric blankets or hot water bottles.

Abrasions
Clean the wound and wash out thoroughly with fresh water; apply antiseptic.

 Remember: an injured dog may attempt to bite a helping hand from fear and confusion. Always muzzle the dog before trying to offer assistance.

can pass on disease resistance to her puppies, which can last for eight to ten weeks. She can also pass on parasites and many infections. That's why it is helpful to learn as much as possible about the health of the dam.

WEANING TO FIVE MONTHS OLD
Puppies should be weaned by the time they are about two months old. A puppy that remains for at least eight weeks with his mother and littermates usually adapts better to other dogs and people in his life.

Sometimes new owners have their puppy examined by a veterinarian immediately, which is a good idea. Vaccination programs usually begin when the puppy is very young. The puppy will have his teeth examined and have his skeletal conformation and general health checked prior to certification by the veterinarian. Puppies in certain breeds have problems

with their kneecaps, cataracts and other eye problems, heart murmurs and undescended testicles. They may also have personality problems and your veterinarian might have training in temperament evaluation.

FIVE MONTHS TO ONE YEAR
Unless you intend to breed or show your dog, neutering the puppy around six months of age is recommended, although opinions vary regarding the best age at which to have this done. Discuss this with your veterinarian. Neutering and spaying have proven to be extremely beneficial to the health of both male and female dogs. Besides eliminating the possibility of pregnancy, it inhibits (but does not prevent) breast cancer in bitches and prostate cancer in male dogs.

DOGS OLDER THAN ONE YEAR
Continue to visit the veterinarian at least once a year. There is no such disease as old age, but bodily functions do change with age. The eyes and ears are no longer as efficient. Liver, kidney and intestinal functions often decline. Proper dietary changes, recommended by your veterinarian, can make life more pleasant for the aging Shih Tzu and you.

VACCINATION SCHEDULING
Most vaccinations are given by injection and should only be done

A FAIR WORMING
Caring for the puppy starts before the puppy is born by keeping the dam healthy and well-nourished. Most puppies have worms, even if they are not evident, so a worming program is essential. The worms continually shed eggs except during their dormant stage, when they just rest in the tissues of the puppy. During this stage they are not evident during a routine examination.

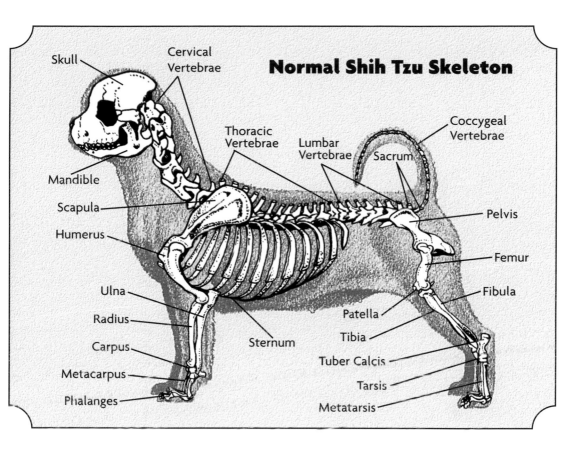

Normal Shih Tzu Skeleton

Skull

Cervical Vertebrae

Thoracic Vertebrae

Lumbar Vertebrae

Sacrum

Coccygeal Vertebrae

Mandible

Scapula

Humerus

Pelvis

Femur

Ulna

Fibula

Radius

Patella

Carpus

Tibia

Sternum

Metacarpus

Tuber Calcis

Phalanges

Tarsis

Metatarsis

by a veterinarian. Both he and you should keep a record of the date of the injection, the identification of the vaccine and the amount given. Some vets give a first vaccination at eight weeks, but most dog breeders prefer the course not to commence until about ten weeks because of the risk of negating any antibodies passed on by the dam. The vaccination scheduling is usually based on a 15-day cycle. You must take your vet's advice as to when to vaccinate as this may differ according to the vaccine used.

Most vaccinations immunize your puppy against viruses. The usual vaccines contain immunizing doses of several different viruses such as distemper, parvovirus, parainfluenza and hepatitis. There are other vaccines available when the puppy is at risk. You should rely upon professional advice. This is especially true for the booster-shot program. Most vaccination programs require a booster when the puppy is a year old and once a year thereafter. In

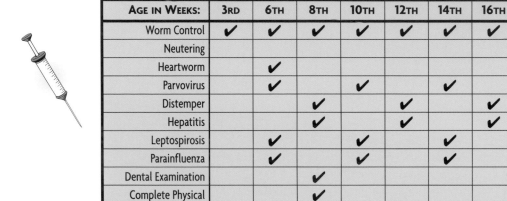

HEALTH AND VACCINATION SCHEDULE

AGE IN WEEKS:	3RD	6TH	8TH	10TH	12TH	14TH	16TH	20-24TH
Worm Control	✔	✔	✔	✔	✔	✔	✔	✔
Neutering								✔
Heartworm		✔						✔
Parvovirus		✔		✔		✔		✔
Distemper			✔		✔		✔	
Hepatitis			✔		✔		✔	
Leptospirosis		✔		✔		✔		
Parainfluenza		✔		✔		✔		
Dental Examination			✔					✔
Complete Physical			✔					✔
Temperament Testing			✔					
Coronavirus					✔			
Kennel Cough		✔						
Hip Dysplasia							✔	
Rabies								✔

Vaccinations are not instantly effective. It takes about two weeks for the dog's immune system to develop antibodies. Most vaccinations require annual booster shots. Your veterinarian should guide you in this regard.

some cases, circumstances may require more or less frequent immunizations.

Kennel cough, more formally known as tracheobronchitis, is treated with a vaccine that is sprayed into the dog's nostrils. Kennel cough is usually included in routine vaccination, but this is often not so effective as for other major diseases.

SKIN PROBLEMS IN SHIH TZU

Veterinarians are consulted by dog owners for skin problems more than for any other group of diseases or maladies. Dogs' skin is almost as sensitive as human skin and both suffer almost the same ailments, though the occurrence of acne in most breeds of dog is rare! For this reason, veterinary dermatology has developed into a specialty practiced by many veterinarians.

Since many skin problems have visual symptoms that are almost identical, it requires the skill of an experienced veterinary dermatologist to identify and cure many of the more severe skin disorders. Pet shops sell many treatments for skin problems, but most of the treatments are directed at symptoms and not the underlying problem(s). If your dog is suffering from a skin disorder, you should seek professional assistance as quickly as possible. As with all diseases, the earlier a problem is identified and treated, the more successful is the cure.

HEREDITARY SKIN DISORDERS
Veterinary dermatologists are currently researching a number of skin disorders that are believed to have a hereditary basis. These inherited diseases are transmitted by both parents, who appear (phenotypically) normal but have a recessive gene for the disease, meaning that they carry, but are not affected by, the disease. These diseases pose serious problems to breeders because in some instances there are no methods of identifying carriers. Often the secondary diseases associated with these skin conditions are even more debilitating than the skin disorders themselves, including cancers and respiratory problems.

Among the hereditary skin disorders, for which the mode of inheritance is known, are cutaneous asthenia (Ehlers-Danlos syndrome), sebaceous adenitis, cyclic hematopoiesis, dermatomyositis, IgA deficiency, color dilution alopecia and nodular dermatofibrosis. All inherited diseases must be diagnosed and treated by a veterinary specialist.

DEWORMING
Ridding your puppy of worms is very important because they remove the nutrients that a growing puppy needs and certain worms that puppies carry, such as tapeworms and roundworms, can also infect humans.

Breeders initiate deworming programs at or about four weeks of age. The routine is repeated every two or three weeks until the puppy is three months old. The breeder from whom you obtained your puppy should provide you with the complete details of the deworming program.

Your veterinarian can prescribe and monitor the rest of the deworming program for you. The usual program is treating the puppy every 15–20 days until the puppy is positively worm-free. It is advised that you only treat your puppy with drugs that are recommended professionally.

PARASITE BITES
Many of us are allergic to insect bites. The bites itch, erupt and may even become infected. Dogs have the same reaction to fleas, ticks and/or mites. When an insect lands on you, you have the chance to whisk it away with your hand. Unfortunately, when your dog is bitten by a flea, tick or mite, he can only scratch it away or bite it. By the time the

DENTAL HEALTH

A dental examination is in order when the dog is between six months and one year of age so that any permanent teeth that have erupted incorrectly can be corrected. It is important to begin a brushing routine at home, using dental-care products made for dogs, such as small tooth-brushes and specially formulated toothpaste. Durable nylon and safe edible chews should be a part of your dog's arsenal for good health, good teeth and pleasant breath. The vast majority of dogs three to four years old and older has diseases of the gums from lack of dental attention. Using the various types of dental chews can be very effective in controlling dental plaque.

dog has been bitten, the parasite has done some of its damage. It may also have laid eggs to cause further problems in the near future. The itching from parasite bites is probably due to the saliva injected into the site when the parasite sucks the dog's blood.

AIRBORNE ALLERGIES

Just as humans have hay fever, rose fever and other fevers from which they suffer during the pollinating season, many dogs suffer from the same allergies. When the pollen count is high, your dog might suffer, but don't expect him to sneeze and have a runny nose as a human would. Dogs react to pollen allergies the same way they react to fleas—they scratch and bite themselves.

Dogs, like humans, can be tested for allergens. Discuss the testing with your veterinary dermatologist.

AUTO-IMMUNE SKIN CONDITIONS

Auto-immune skin conditions are commonly referred to as being allergic to yourself, while allergies are usually inflammatory reactions to an outside stimulus. Auto-immune diseases cause serious damage to the tissues that are involved.

The best known auto-immune disease is lupus, which affects people as well as dogs. The symptoms are variable and may affect the kidneys, bones, blood chemistry and skin. It can be fatal to both dogs and humans, though it is not thought to be transmissible. It is usually successfully treated with cortisone, prednisone or similar corticosteroid, but extensive use of these drugs can have harmful side effects.

FOOD PROBLEMS
FOOD ALLERGIES

Dogs are allergic to many foods that are best-sellers and highly recommended by breeders and veterinarians. Changing the brand of food that you buy may not eliminate the problem if the element to which the dog is allergic is contained in the new brand.

Recognizing a food allergy is difficult. Humans vomit or have rashes when they eat a food to which they are allergic. Dogs neither vomit nor (usually) develop a rash. They react in the same manner as they do to an airborne or flea allergy: they itch, scratch and bite, thus making the diagnosis extremely difficult. While pollen allergies and para-

site bites are usually seasonal, food allergies are year-round problems.

FOOD INTOLERANCE

Food intolerance is the inability of the dog to completely digest certain foods. For example, puppies that may have done very well on their mother's milk may not do well on cow's milk. The result of this food intolerance may be evident in the form of loose bowels, passing gas and stomach pains. These are the only obvious symptoms of food intolerance and that makes diagnosis difficult.

Disease	What is it?	What causes it?	Symptoms
Leptospirosis	Severe disease that affects the internal organs; can be spread to people.	A bacterium, which is often carried by rodents, that enters through mucous membranes and spreads quickly throughout the body.	Range from fever, vomiting and loss of appetite in less severe cases to shock, irreversible kidney damage and possibly death in most severe cases.
Rabies	Potentially deadly virus that infects warm-blooded mammals.	Bite from a carrier of the virus, mainly wild animals.	1st stage: dog exhibits change in behavior, fear. 2nd stage: dog's behavior becomes more aggressive. 3rd stage: loss of coordination, trouble with bodily functions.
Parvovirus	Highly contagious virus, potentially deadly.	Ingestion of the virus, which is usually spread through the feces of infected dogs.	Most common: severe diarrhea. Also vomiting, fatigue, lack of appetite.
Kennel cough	Contagious respiratory infection.	Combination of types of bacteria and virus. Most common: *Bordetella bronchiseptica* bacteria and parainfluenza virus.	Chronic cough.
Distemper	Disease primarily affecting respiratory and nervous system.	Virus that is related to the human measles virus.	Mild symptoms such as fever, lack of appetite and mucus secretion progress to evidence of brain damage, "hard pad."
Hepatitis	Virus primarily affecting the liver.	Canine adenovirus type I (CAV-1). Enters system when dog breathes in particles.	Lesser symptoms include listlessness, diarrhea, vomiting. More severe symptoms include "blue-eye" (clumps of virus in eye).
Coronavirus	Virus resulting in digestive problems.	Virus is spread through infected dog's feces.	Stomach upset evidenced by lack of appetite, vomiting, diarrhea.

TREATING FOOD PROBLEMS

It is possible to handle food allergies and food intolerance yourself. Put your dog on a diet that he has never had. Obviously if he has never eaten this new food he can't yet have been allergic or intolerant of it. Start with a single ingredient that is not in the dog's diet at the present time. Ingredients like chopped beef or chicken are common in dog's diets, so try something like fish, lamb, rabbit or another protein source. Keep the dog on this diet (with no additives) for a month. If the symptoms of food allergy or intolerance disappear, chances are your dog has a food allergy.

Don't think that the single ingredient cured the problem. You still must find a suitable diet and ascertain which ingredient in the old diet was objectionable. This is most easily done by adding ingredients to the new diet one at a

POISONOUS PLANTS

Below is a partial list of plants that are considered poisonous. These plants can cause skin irritation, illness and even death. You should be aware of the types of plants that grow in your garden and that you keep in your home. Special care should be taken to rid your garden of dangerous plants and to keep all plants in the household out of your Shih Tzu's reach.

American Blue Flag	False Acacia	Mistletoe (berries)
Bachelor's Button	Fern	Monkshood
Barberry	Foxglove	Mullein
Bog Iris	Hellebore	Narcissus
Boxwood	Herb of Grace	Peony
Buttercup	Holly	Persian Ivy
Cherry Pits	Horse Chestnut	Rhododendron
Chinese Arbor	Iris (bulb)	Rhubarb
Chokecherry	Japanese Yew	Shallon
Christmas Rose	Jerusalem Cherry	Solomon's Seal
Climbing Lily	Jimson Weed	Star of Bethlehem
Crown of Thorns	Lenten Rose	Water Lily
Elderberry (berries)	Lily of the Valley	Wood Spurge
Elephant Ear	Marigold	Wisteria
English Ivy	Milkwort	Yew

time. Let the dog stay on the modified diet for a month before you add another ingredient. Eventually, you will determine the ingredient that caused the adverse reaction.

An alternative method is to carefully study the ingredients in the diet to which your dog is allergic or intolerant. Identify the main ingredient in this diet and eliminate the main ingredient by buying a different food that does not have that ingredient. Keep

FAT OR FICTION?
The myth that dogs need extra fat in their diets can be harmful. Should your vet recommend extra fat, use safflower oil instead of animal oils. Safflower oil has been shown to be less likely to cause allergic reactions.

experimenting until the symptoms disappear after one month on the new diet.

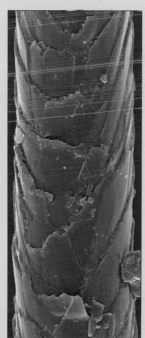
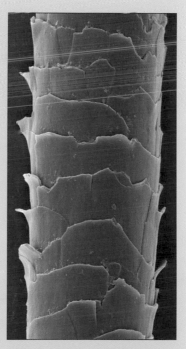

S.E.M. MICROGRAPHS BY DR DENNIS KUNKEL, UNIVERSITY OF HAWAII

One of the fine hairs of the Shih Tzu, highly enlarged.

A dying hair starting to disintegrate. Hairs like this are usually brushed out in the daily grooming process.

Thick, heavy hair in perfect condition.

A male dog flea, *Ctenocephalides canis.*

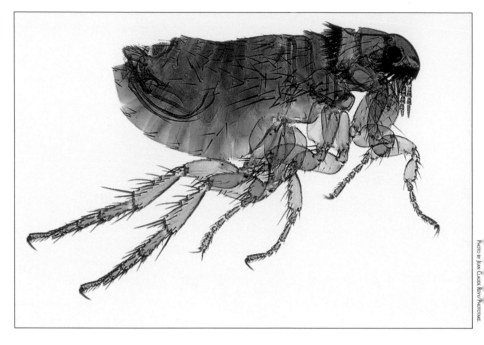

PHOTO BY JEAN CLAUDE REVY/PHOTOTAKE

EXTERNAL PARASITES
FLEAS
Of all the problems to which dogs are prone, none is more well known and frustrating than fleas. Flea infestation is relatively simple to cure but difficult to prevent. Parasites that are harbored inside the body are a bit more difficult to eradicate but they are easier to control.

To control flea infestation, you have to understand the flea's life cycle. Fleas are often thought of as a summertime problem, but centrally heated homes have changed the patterns and fleas can be found at any time of the year. The most effective method of flea control is a two-stage approach: one stage to kill the adult fleas, and the other to control the development of pre-adult fleas. Unfortunately, no single active ingredient is effective against all stages of the life cycle.

FLEA KILLER CAUTION— "POISON"
Flea-killers are poisonous. You should not spray these toxic chemicals on areas of a dog's body that he licks, including his genitals and his face. Flea killers taken internally are a better answer, but check with your vet in case internal therapy is not advised for your dog.

LIFE CYCLE STAGES

During its life, a flea will pass through four life stages: egg, larva, pupa or nymph and adult. The adult stage is the most visible and irritating stage of the flea life cycle, and this is why the majority of flea-control products concentrate on this stage. The fact is that adult fleas account for only 1% of the total flea population, and the other 99% exist in pre-adult stages, i.e., eggs, larvae and nymphs. The pre-adult stages are barely visible to the naked eye.

THE LIFE CYCLE OF THE FLEA

Eggs are laid on the dog, usually in quantities of about 20 or 30, several times a day. The adult female flea must have a blood meal before each egg-laying session. When first laid, the eggs will cling to the dog's hair, as the eggs are still moist. However, they will quickly dry out and fall from the dog, especially if the dog moves around or scratches. Many eggs will fall off in the dog's favorite area or an area in which he spends a lot of time, such as his bed.

Once the eggs fall from the dog onto the carpet or furniture, they will hatch into larvae. This takes from one to ten days. Larvae are not particularly mobile and will usually travel only a few inches from where they hatch. However, they do have a tendency to move away from bright light and heavy

EN GARDE:
CATCHING FLEAS OFF GUARD!
Consider the following ways to arm yourself against fleas:
- Add a small amount of pennyroyal or eucalyptus oil to your dog's bath. These natural remedies repel fleas.
- Supplement your dog's food with fresh garlic (minced or grated) and a hearty amount of brewer's yeast, both of which ward off fleas.
- Use a flea comb on your dog daily. Submerge fleas in a cup of bleach to kill them quickly.
- Confine the dog to only a few rooms to limit the spread of fleas in the home.
- Vacuum daily...and get all of the crevices! Dispose of the bag every few days until the problem is under control.
- Wash your dog's bedding daily. Cover cushions where your dog sleeps with towels, and wash the towels often.

traffic—under furniture and behind doors are common places to find high quantities of flea larvae.

The flea larvae feed on dead organic matter, including adult flea feces, until they are ready to change into adult fleas. Fleas will usually remain as larvae for around seven days. After this period, the larvae will pupate into protective pupae. While inside the pupae, the larvae will undergo

metamorphosis and change into
adult fleas. This can take as little
time as a few days, but the adult
fleas can remain inside the pupae
waiting to hatch for up to two
years. The pupae are signaled to
hatch by certain stimuli, such as
physical pressure—the pupae's
being stepped on, heat from an
animal's lying on the pupae or
increased carbon-dioxide levels
and vibrations—indicating that a
suitable host is available.

Once hatched, the adult flea
must feed within a few days.
Once the adult flea finds a host, it
will not leave voluntarily. It only
becomes dislodged by grooming
or the host animal's scratching.

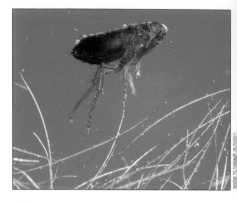

The adult flea will remain on the
host for the duration of its life
unless forcibly removed.

TREATING THE ENVIRONMENT AND THE DOG

Treating fleas should be a two-
pronged attack. First, the
environment needs to be treated;
this includes carpets and
furniture, especially the dog's
bedding and areas underneath
furniture. The environment
should be treated with a
household spray containing an
Insect Growth Regulator (IGR) and
an insecticide to kill the adult
fleas. Most IGRs are effective
against eggs and larvae; they
actually mimic the fleas' own
hormones and stop the eggs and
larvae from developing into adult
fleas. There are currently no
treatments available to attack the
pupa stage of the life cycle, so the
adult insecticide is used to kill
the newly hatched adult fleas
before they find a host. Most IGRs
are active for many months, while

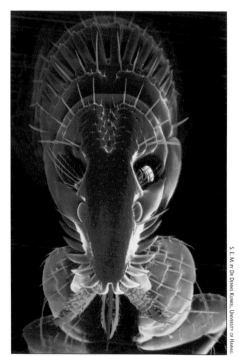

S. E. M. by Dr. Dennis Kunkel, University of Hawaii

THE LIFE CYCLE OF THE FLEA

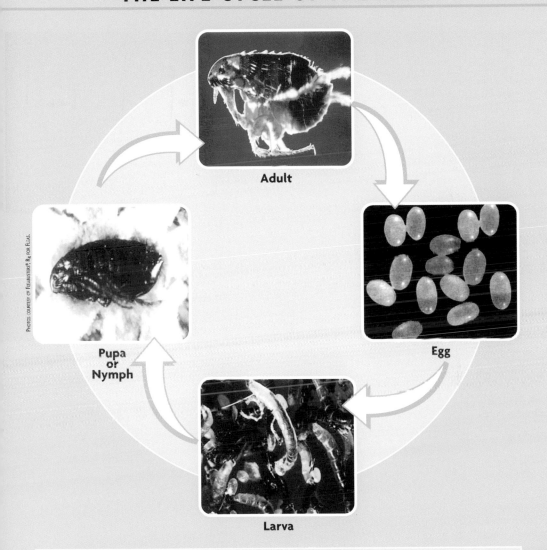

Adult

Egg

Larva

Pupa or Nymph

A LOOK AT FLEAS
Fleas have been around for millions of years and have adapted to changing host animals. They are able to go through a complete life cycle in less than one month or they can extend their lives to almost two years by remaining as pupae or cocoons. They do not need blood or any other food for up to 20 months.

> **INSECT GROWTH REGULATOR (IGR)**
>
> Two types of products should be used when treating fleas—a product to treat the pet and a product to treat the home. Adult fleas represent less than 1% of the flea population. The pre-adult fleas (eggs, larvae and pupae) represent more than 99% of the flea population and are found in the environment; it is in the case of pre-adult fleas that products containing an Insect Growth Regulator (IGR) should be used in the home.
>
> IGRs are a new class of compounds used to prevent the development of insects. They do not kill the insect outright, but instead use the insect's biology against it to stop it from completing its growth. Products that contain methoprene are the world's first and leading IGRs. Used to control fleas and other insects, this type of IGR will stop flea larvae from developing and protect the house for up to seven months.

The American dog tick, *Dermacentor variabilis*, is probably the most common tick found on dogs. Look at the strength in its eight legs! No wonder it's hard to detach them.

adult insecticides are only active for a few days.

When treating with a household spray, it is a good idea to vacuum before applying the product. This stimulates as many pupae as possible to hatch into adult fleas. The vacuum cleaner should also be treated with an insecticide to prevent the eggs and larvae that have been collected in the vacuum bag from hatching.

The second stage of treatment is to apply an adult insecticide to the dog. Traditionally, this would be in the form of a collar or a spray, but more recent innovations include digestible insecticides that poison the fleas when they ingest the dog's blood. Alternatively, there are drops that, when placed on the back of the dog's neck, spread throughout the hair and skin to kill adult fleas.

TICKS

Though not as common as fleas, ticks are found all over the tropical and temperate world. They don't bite, like fleas; they harpoon. They dig their sharp proboscis (nose) into the dog's skin and drink the blood. Their

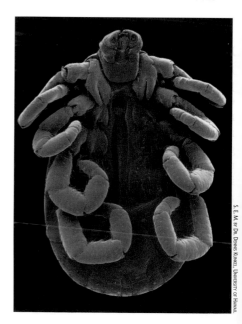

S. E. M. BY DR. DENNIS KUNKEL, UNIVERSITY OF HAWAII

only food and drink is dog's blood. Dogs can get Lyme disease, Rocky Mountain spotted fever, tick bite paralysis and many other diseases from ticks. They may live where fleas are found and they like to hide in cracks or seams in walls. They are controlled the same way fleas are controlled.

The American dog tick, *Dermacentor variabilis*, may well be the most common dog tick in many geographical areas, especially those areas where the climate is hot and humid. Most dog ticks have life expectancies of a week to six months, depending upon climatic conditions. They can neither jump nor fly, but they can crawl slowly and can range up to 16 feet to reach a sleeping or unsuspecting dog.

MITES
Just as fleas and ticks can be problematic for your dog, mites can also lead to an itchy nuisance. Microscopic in size, mites are related to ticks and generally take up permanent residence on their host animal—in this case, your dog! The term *mange* refers to any infestation caused by one of the mighty mites, of which there are six varieties that concern dog owners.

Demodex mites cause a condition known as demodicosis

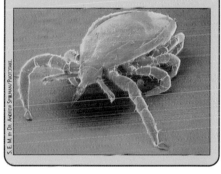

DEER-TICK CROSSING
The great outdoors may be fun for your dog, but it also is a home to dangerous ticks. Deer ticks carry a bacterium known as *Borrelia burgdorferi* and are most active in the autumn and spring. When infections are caught early, penicillin and tetracycline are effective antibiotics, but if left untreated the bacteria may cause neurological, kidney and cardiac problems as well as long-term trouble with walking and painful joints.

S.E.M. BY DR. ANDREW SYRED/PHOTOTAKE

PHOTO BY DR. DENNIS KUNKEL, UNIVERSITY OF HAWAII

The head of an American dog tick, *Dermacentor variabilis*, enlarged and colorized for effect.

125

The mange mite, *Psoroptes bovis*, can infest cattle and other domestic animals.

(sometimes called red mange or follicular mange), in which the mites live in the dog's hair follicles and sebaceous glands in larger-than-normal amounts. This type of mange is commonly passed from the dam to her puppies and usually shows up on the puppies' muzzles, though demodicosis is not transferable from one normal dog to another. Most dogs recover from this type of mange without any treatment, though topical therapies are commonly prescribed by the vet.

Human lice look like dog lice; the two are closely related.

PHOTO BY DWIGHT R. KUHN.

The *Cheyletiellosis* mite is the hook-mouthed culprit associated with "walking dandruff," a condition that affects dogs as well as cats and rabbits. This mite lives on the surface of the animal's skin and is readily transferable through direct or indirect contact with an affected animal. The dandruff is present in the form of scaly skin, which may or may not be itchy. If not treated, this mange can affect a whole kennel of dogs and can be spread to humans as well.

The *Sarcoptes* mite causes intense itching on the dog in the form of a condition known as scabies or sarcoptic mange. The cycle of the *Sarcoptes* mite lasts about three weeks, and the mites live in the top layer of the dog's skin (epidermis), preferably in areas with little hair. Scabies is highly contagious and can be passed to humans. Sometimes an allergic reaction to the mite worsens the severe itching associated with sarcoptic mange.

Ear mites, *Otodectes cynotis,* lead to otodectic mange, which most commonly affects the outer ear canal of the dog, though other areas can be affected as well. Dogs with ear-mite infestation commonly scratch at their ears, causing further irritation, and shake their heads. Dark brown droppings in the outer ear confirm the diagnosis. Your vet can prescribe a treatment to flush out the ears and kill any eggs in the ears. A complete month of treatment is necessary to cure the mange.

Two other mites, less common in dogs, include *Dermanyssus gallinae* (the poultry or red mite) and *Eutrombicula alfreddugesi* (the North American mite associated with trombiculidiasis or chigger infestation). The poultry mite frequently lives on chickens, but can transfer to dogs who spend time near farm animals. Chigger infestation affects dogs in the

DO NOT MIX
Never mix pest control products without first consulting your vet. Some products can become toxic when combined with others and can cause fatal consequences.

NOT A DROP TO DRINK
Never allow your dog to swim in polluted water or public areas where water quality can be suspect. Even perfectly clear water can harbor parasites, many of which can cause serious to fatal illnesses in canines. Areas inhabited by water-fowl and other wildlife are especially dangerous.

Central US who have exposure to woodlands. The types of mange caused by both of these mites are treatable by veterinarians.

INTERNAL PARASITES
Most animals—fishes, birds and mammals, including dogs and humans—have worms and other parasites that live inside their bodies. According to Dr. Herbert R. Axelrod, the fish pathologist, there are two kinds of parasites: dumb and smart. The smart parasites live in peaceful cooperation with their hosts (symbiosis), while the dumb parasites kill their hosts. Most worm infections are relatively easy to control. If they are not controlled, they weaken the host dog to the point that other medical problems occur, but they do not kill the host as dumb parasites would.

A brown dog tick, *Rhipicephalus sanguineus*, is an uncommon but annoying tick found on dogs.

PHOTO BY CAROLINA BIOLOGICAL SUPPLY/PHOTOTAKE.

127

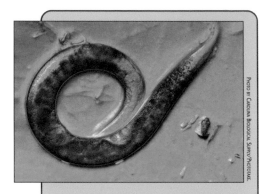

The roundworm *Rhabditis* can infect both dogs and humans.

The roundworm, *Ascaris lumbricoides*.

ROUNDWORMS

Average-size dogs can pass 1,360,000 roundworm eggs every day. For example, if there were only 1 million dogs in the world, the world would be saturated with thousands of tons of dog feces. These feces would contain around 15,000,000,000 roundworm eggs.

Up to 31% of home yards and children's sand boxes in the US contain roundworm eggs.

Flushing dog's feces down the toilet is not a safe practice because the usual sewage treatments do not destroy roundworm eggs.

Infected puppies start shedding roundworm eggs at three weeks of age. They can be infected by their mother's milk.

ROUNDWORMS

The roundworms that infect dogs are known scientifically as *Toxocara canis*. They live in the dog's intestines and shed eggs continually. It has been estimated that a dog produces about 6 or more ounces of feces every day. Each ounce of feces averages hundreds of thousands of roundworm eggs. There are no known areas in which dogs roam that do not contain roundworm eggs. The greatest danger of roundworms is that they infect people, too! It is wise to have your dog tested regularly for roundworms.

In young puppies, roundworms cause bloated bellies, diarrhea, coughing and vomiting, and are transmitted from the dam (through blood or milk). Affected puppies will not appear as animated as normal puppies. The worms appear spaghetti-like, measuring as long as 6 inches. Adult dogs can acquire roundworms through coprophagia (eating contaminated feces) or by killing rodents that carry roundworms.

Roundworm infection can kill puppies and cause severe problems in adults, as the hatched larvae travel to the lungs and trachea through the bloodstream. Cleanliness is the best preventative for roundworms. Always pick up after your dog and dispose of feces in appropriate receptacles.

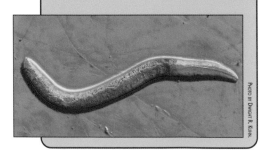

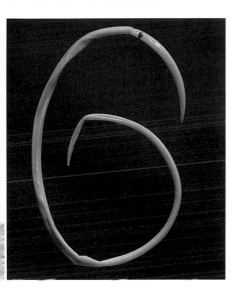

HOOKWORMS

In the United States, dog owners have to be concerned about four different species of hookworm, the most common and most serious of which is *Ancylostoma caninum,* which prefers warm climates. The others are *Ancylostoma braziliense, Ancylostoma tubaeforme* and *Uncinaria stenocephala,* the latter of which is a concern to dogs living in the Northern US and Canada, as this species prefers cold climates. Hookworms are dangerous to humans as well as to dogs and cats, and can be the cause of severe anemia due to iron deficiency. The worm uses its teeth to attach itself to the dog's intestines and changes the site of its attachment about six times per day. Each time the worm repositions itself, the dog loses blood and can become anemic. *Ancylostoma caninum* is the most likely of the four species to cause anemia in the dog.

Symptoms of hookworm infection include dark stools, weight loss, general weakness, pale coloration and anemia, as well as possible skin problems. Fortunately, hookworms are easily purged from the affected dog with a number of medications that have proven effective. Discuss these with your veterinarian. Most heartworm preventatives include a hookworm insecticide as well.

Owners also must be aware that hookworms can infect humans, who can acquire the larvae through exposure to contaminated feces. Since the worms cannot complete their life cycle on a human, the worms simply infest the skin and cause irritation. This condition is known as cutaneous larva migrans syndrome. As a preventative, use disposable gloves or a "poop-scoop" to pick up your dog's droppings and prevent your dog (or neighborhood cats) from defecating in children's play areas.

The hookworm, *Ancylostoma caninum.*

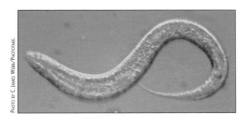

The infective stage of the hookworm larva.

PHOTO BY C. JAMES WEBB/PHOTOTAKE

TAPEWORMS

Humans, rats, squirrels, foxes, coyotes, wolves and domestic dogs are all susceptible to tapeworm infection. Except in humans, tapeworms are usually not a fatal infection. Infected individuals can harbor 1000 parasitic worms.

Tapeworms, like some other types of worm, are hermaphroditic, meaning male and female in the same worm.

If dogs eat infected rats or mice, or anything else infected with tapeworm, they get the tapeworm disease. One month after attaching to a dog's intestine, the worm starts shedding eggs. These eggs are infective immediately. Infective eggs can live for a few months without a host animal.

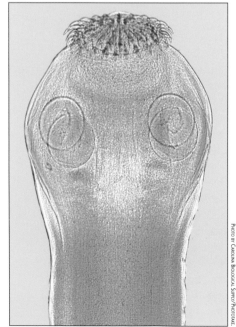

The head and rostellum (the round prominence on the scolex) of a tapeworm, which infects dogs and humans.

PHOTO BY CAROLINA BIOLOGICAL SUPPLY/PHOTOTAKE.

TAPEWORMS

There are many species of tapeworm, all of which are carried by fleas! The most common tapeworm affecting dogs is known as *Dipylidium caninum*. The dog eats the flea and starts the tapeworm cycle. Humans can also be infected with tapeworms—so don't eat fleas! Fleas are so small that your dog could pass them onto your hands, your plate or your food and thus make it possible for you to ingest a flea that is carrying tapeworm eggs.

While tapeworm infection is not life-threatening in dogs (smart parasite!), it can be the cause of a very serious liver disease for humans. About 50% of the humans infected with *Echinococcus multilocularis*, a type of tapeworm that causes alveolar hydatid, perish.

WHIPWORMS

In North America, whipworms are counted among the most common parasitic worms in dogs. The whipworm's scientific name is *Trichuris vulpis*. These worms attach themselves in the lower parts of the intestine, where they feed. Affected dogs may only experience upset tummies, colic and diarrhea. These worms, however, can live for months or years in the dog, beginning their larval stage in the small intestine, spending their adult stage in the large intestine and finally passing infective eggs through the dog's feces. The only way to detect whipworms is through a fecal examination, though this is not always foolproof. Treatment for whipworms is tricky, due to the worms' unusual life-cycle pattern, and very often dogs are reinfected due to exposure to infective eggs on the ground. The whipworm eggs can survive in the environment for as long as five years, thus cleaning up droppings in your own backyard as well as in public places is absolutely essential for sanitation purposes and the health of your dog.

THREADWORMS

Though less common than round-worms, hookworms and others already mentioned, threadworms concern dog owners in the Southwestern US and Gulf Coast area where the climate is hot and humid. Living in the small intestine of the dog, this worm measures a mere 2 millimeters and is round in shape. Like that of the whipworm, the threadworm's life cycle is very complex and the eggs and larvae are passed through the feces. A deadly disease in humans, *Strongyloides* readily infects people, and the handling of feces is the most common means of trans-mission. Threadworms are most often seen in young puppies; bloody diarrhea and pneumonia are symptoms. Sick puppies must be isolated and treated immediately; vets recommend a follow-up treat-ment one month later.

HEARTWORM PREVENTATIVES

There are many heartworm preventatives on the market, many of which are sold at your veterinarian's office. These products can be given daily or monthly, depending on the manufacturer's instructions. All of these preventatives contain chemical insecticides directed at killing heartworms, which leads to some controversy among dog owners. In effect, heartworm preventatives are neces-sary evils, though you should determine how necessary based on your pet's lifestyle. There is no doubt that heartworm is a dreadful disease that threatens the lives of dogs. However, the likelihood of your dog's being bitten by an infected mosquito is slim in most places, and a mosquito-repellent (or an herbal remedy such as Wormwood or Black Walnut) is much safer for your dog and will not compromise his immune system (the way heartworm preventatives will). Should you decide to use the tradi-tional preventative "medications," you can consider giving the pill every other or third month. Since the toxins in the pill will kill the heartworms at all stages of develop-ment, the pill would be effective in killing larvae, nymphs or adults and it takes four months for the larvae to reach the adult stage. Thus, there is no rationale to poison-ing the dog's system on a monthly basis. Lastly, do not give the pill during the winter months since there are no mosquitoes around to pass on their infection, unless you live in a tropical environment.

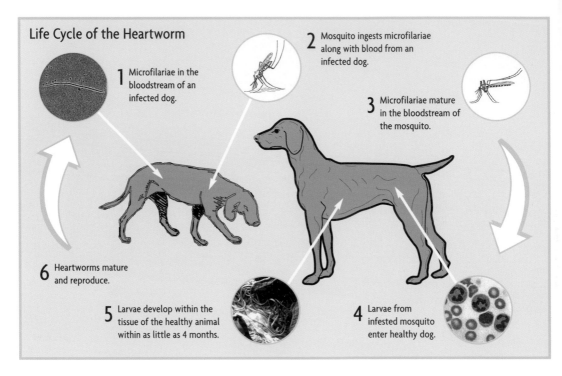

Life Cycle of the Heartworm

1 Microfilariae in the bloodstream of an infected dog.

2 Mosquito ingests microfilariae along with blood from an infected dog.

3 Microfilariae mature in the bloodstream of the mosquito.

4 Larvae from infested mosquito enter healthy dog.

5 Larvae develop within the tissue of the healthy animal within as little as 4 months.

6 Heartworms mature and reproduce.

HEARTWORMS

Heartworms are thin, extended worms up to 12 inches long, which live in a dog's heart and the major blood vessels surrounding it. Dogs may have up to 200 worms. Symptoms may be loss of energy, loss of appetite, coughing, the development of a pot belly and anemia.

Heartworms are transmitted by mosquitoes. The mosquito drinks the blood of an infected dog and takes in larvae with the blood. The larvae, called microfilariae, develop within the body of the mosquito and are passed on to the next dog bitten after the larvae mature. It takes two to three weeks for the larvae to develop to the infective stage within the body of the mosquito. Dogs are usually treated at about six weeks of age and maintained on a prophylactic dose given monthly.

Blood testing for heartworms is not necessarily indicative of how seriously your dog is infected. Although this is a dangerous disease, it is not easy for a dog to be infected. Discuss the various preventatives with your vet, as there are many different types now available. Together you can decide on a safe course of prevention for your dog.

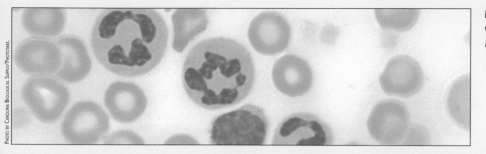

Magnified heart-worm larvae, *Dirofilaria immitis.*

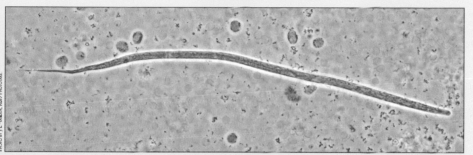

Heartworm, *Dirofilaria immitis.*

The heart of a dog infected with canine heart-worm, *Dirofilaria immitis.*

CDS: COGNITIVE DYSFUNCTION SYNDROME
"Old-Dog Syndrome"

There are many ways for you to evaluate old-dog syndrome. Veterinarians have defined CDS (cognitive dysfunction syndrome) as the gradual deterioration of cognitive abilities. These are indicated by changes in the dog's behavior. When a dog changes his routine response, and maladies have been eliminated as the cause of these behavioral changes, then CDS is the usual diagnosis.

More than half the dogs over eight years old suffer from some form of CDS. The older the dog, the more chance he has of suffering from CDS. In humans, doctors often dismiss the CDS behavioral changes as part of "winding down."

There are four major signs of CDS: frequent potty accidents inside the home, sleeping much more or much less than normal, acting confused and failing to respond to social stimuli.

SYMPTOMS OF CDS

FREQUENT POTTY ACCIDENTS
- *Urinates in the house.*
- *Defecates in the house.*
- *Doesn't signal that he wants to go out.*

SLEEP PATTERNS
- *Takes longer to awaken.*
- *Sleeps more than normal during the day.*
- *Sleeps less during the night.*

CONFUSION
- *Goes outside and just stands there.*
- *Appears confused with a faraway look in his eyes.*
- *Hides more often.*
- *Doesn't recognize friends.*
- *Doesn't come when called.*
- *Walks around listlessly and without a destination.*

FAILURE TO RESPOND TO SOCIAL STIMULI
- *Comes to people less frequently, whether called or not.*
- *Doesn't tolerate petting for more than a short time.*
- *Doesn't come to the door when you return home.*

Shih Tzu

The term *old* is a qualitative term. For dogs, as well as their masters, old is relative. Certainly we can all distinguish between a puppy Shih Tzu and an adult Shih Tzu— there are the obvious physical traits, such as size, appearance and facial expressions, and personality traits. Puppies and young dogs like to play with children. Children's natural exuberance is a good match for the seemingly endless energy of young dogs. They like to run, jump, chase and retrieve. When dogs grow up and cease their interaction with children, they are often thought of as being too old to play with the kids.

On the other hand, if a Shih Tzu is only exposed to people with quieter lifestyles, his life will normally be less active and the decrease in his activity level as he ages will not be as obvious.

If people live to be 100 years old, dogs live to be 20 years old. While this may be a rule of thumb, it is very inaccurate. When trying to compare dog years to human years, you cannot make a generalization about all dogs. You can make the generalization that 15 years is a good lifespan for a Shih Tzu, which is quite good compared to many other pure-bred dogs that may only live to 8 or 9 years of age. Some Shih Tzu have been known to live to 20 years. Dogs are generally considered mature within three years, but they can reproduce even earlier. So the first three years of a dog's life are like seven times that of comparable humans. That means a 3-year-old dog is like a 21-year-old human. As the curve of comparison shows, there is no hard and fast rule for comparing dog and human ages. The comparison is made even more difficult,

> ### GETTING OLD
> The bottom line is simply that your dog is getting old when you think he is getting old because he slows down in his level of general activity, including walking, running, eating, jumping and retrieving. On the other hand, the frequency of certain activities increases, such as more sleeping, more barking and more repetition of habits like going to the door without being called when you put your coat on to leave the house.

for not all humans and not all dogs age at the same rate.

WHAT TO LOOK FOR IN SENIORS

Most veterinarians and behaviorists use the seven-year mark as the time to consider a dog a "senior." This term does not imply that the dog is geriatric and has begun to fail in mind and body. Aging is essentially a slowing process. Humans readily admit that they feel a difference in their activity level from age 20 to 30, and then from 30 to 40, etc. By treating the seven-year-old dog as a senior, owners are able to implement certain thera-peutic and preventative medical strategies with the help of their veterinarians. A senior-care program should include at least two veterinary visits per year and screening sessions to determine the dog's health status, as well as nutritional counseling. Veterinarians determine the senior dog's health status through a blood smear for a complete blood count, serum chemistry profile with electrolytes, urinalysis, blood pressure check, electrocardiogram, ocular tonometry (pressure on the eyeball) and dental prophylaxis.

Such an extensive program for senior dogs is well advised before

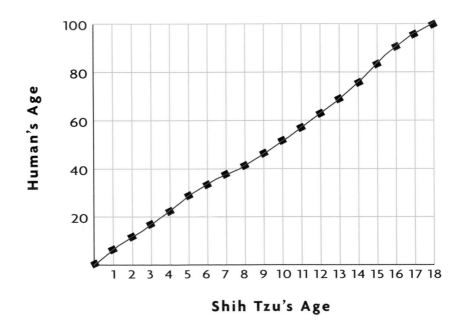

Human's Age / Shih Tzu's Age

Introducing a second dog into the household with an older Shih Tzu can give the senior new-found energies and motivations. Owners must be sure to lavish equal attention on both dogs.

owners start to see the obvious physical signs of aging, such as slower and inhibited movement, graying, increased sleep/nap periods and disinterest in play and other activity. This preventative program promises a longer, healthier life for the aging dog. Among the physical problems common in aging dogs are the loss of sight and hearing, arthritis, kidney and liver failure, diabetes mellitus, heart disease and Cushing's disease (a hormonal disease).

In addition to the physical manifestations discussed, there are some behavioral changes and

SENIOR SIGNS
An old dog starts to show one or more of the following symptoms:
• The hair on the face and paws starts to turn gray. The color breakdown usually starts around the eyes and mouth.
• Sleep patterns are deeper and longer, and the old dog is harder to awaken.
• Food intake diminishes.
• Responses to calls, whistles and other signals are ignored more and more.
• Eye contact does not evoke tail wagging (assuming it once did).

problems related to aging dogs. Dogs suffering from hearing or vision loss, dental discomfort or arthritis can become aggressive. Likewise, the near-deaf and/or blind dog may be startled more easily and react in an unexpectedly aggressive manner. Seniors suffering from senility can become more impatient and irritable. Housesoiling accidents are associated with loss of mobility, kidney problems and loss of sphincter control as well as plaque accumu-

NOTICING THE SYMPTOMS
The symptoms listed below are symptoms that gradually appear and become more noticeable. They are not life-threatening; however, the symptoms below are to be taken very seriously and warrant a discussion with your veterinarian:
• Your dog cries and whimpers when he moves, and he stops running completely.
• Convulsions start or become more serious and frequent. The usual convulsion (spasm) is when the dog stiffens and starts to tremble, being unable or unwilling to move. The seizure usually lasts for 5 to 30 minutes.
• Your dog drinks more water and urinates more frequently. Wetting and bowel accidents take place indoors without warning.
• Vomiting becomes more and more frequent.

lation, physiological brain changes and reactions to medications. Older dogs, just like young puppies, suffer from separation anxiety, which can lead to excessive barking, whining, housesoiling and destructive behavior. Seniors may become fearful of everyday sounds, such as vacuum cleaners, heaters, thunder and passing traffic. Some dogs have difficulty sleeping, due to discomfort, the need for frequent potty visits and the like. Owners should avoid spoiling the older dog with too many fatty treats. Obesity is a common problem in older dogs and subtracts years from their lives. Keep the senior dog as trim as possible since excess weight puts additional stress on the body's vital organs. Some breeders recommend supplementing the diet with foods high in fiber and lower in calories. Adding fresh vegetables and marrow broth to the senior's diet makes a tasty, low-calorie, low-fat supplement. Vets also offer specialty diets for senior dogs that are worth exploring.

Your dog, as he nears his twilight years, needs your patience and good care more than ever. Never punish an older dog for an accident or abnormal behavior. For all the years of love, protection and companionship that your dog has provided, he deserves special attention and courtesies. The older dog may need to relieve himself at 3 a.m.

very obvious that you love your Shih Tzu or you would not be reading this book. Putting a loved dog to sleep is extremely difficult. It is a decision that must be made with your veterinarian. You are usually forced to make the decision when one of the life-threatening symptoms listed above becomes serious enough for you to seek veterinary help. If the prognosis of the malady indicates the end is near and your beloved pet will only suffer more and experience no enjoyment for the balance of his life, then euthanasia is the right choice.

The Shih Tzu owner must take care that his senior dog has appropriate veterinary attention. To ensure your senior's continued good health, twice-annual checkups are advised.

because he can no longer hold it for eight hours. Older dogs may not be able to remain crated for more than two or three hours. It may be time to give up a sofa or chair to your old friend. Although he may not seem as enthusiastic about your attention and petting, he does appreciate the considerations you offer as he gets older.

Your Shih Tzu does not understand why his world is slowing down. Owners must make their dogs' transition into the golden years as pleasant and rewarding as possible.

WHAT TO DO WHEN THE TIME COMES

You are never fully prepared to make a rational decision about putting your dog to sleep. It is

EUTHANASIA

Euthanasia derives from the Greek, meaning "good death." In other words, it is the planned,

CONSISTENCY COUNTS

Puppies and older dogs are very similar in their need for consistency in their lives. Older pets may experience hearing and vision loss, or may just be more easily confused by changes in their homes. Try to keep things consistent for the senior dog. For example, doors that are always open or closed should remain so. Most importantly, don't dismiss a pet just because he's getting old; most senior dogs remain active and important parts of their owners' lives.

painless killing of a dog suffering from a painful, incurable condition, or who is so aged that he cannot walk, see, eat or control his excretory functions.

Euthanasia is usually accomplished by injection with an overdose of an anesthesia or barbiturate. Aside from the prick of the needle, the experience is usually painless.

The decision to euthanize your dog is never easy. The days during which the dog becomes ill and the end occurs can be unusually stressful for you. If this is your first experience with the death of a loved one, you may need the comfort dictated by your religious beliefs. If you are the head of the family and have children, you should have involved them in the decision of putting your Shih Tzu to sleep. Usually your dog can be maintained on drugs for a few days in order to give you ample time to make a decision. During this time, talking with members of your family or even people who have lived through this same experience can ease the burden of your inevitable decision.

Some owners go to great expense to memorialize their departed pets. This statue is a grave marker in a pet cemetery.

THE FINAL RESTING PLACE

Dogs can have some of the same privileges as humans. Your dog can be buried in his entirety in a pet cemetery, which is generally expensive. If he has died at home, he can be buried in your yard in a place suitably marked with a stone or newly planted tree or bush. Alternatively, your dog can be cremated and the ashes returned to you. Some people prefer to leave their dogs at the vet's office for the vet to dispose of.

All of these options should be discussed frankly and openly with your veterinarian. Do not be afraid to ask financial questions. For example, cremations can be individual, but a less expensive option is mass cremation, although of course the ashes cannot then be returned. Vets can

EUTHANASIA

Euthanasia must be performed by a licensed veterinarian. There also may be societies for the prevention of cruelty to animals in your area. They often offer this service upon a vet's recommendation.

usually arrange cremation or burial services on your behalf.

GETTING ANOTHER DOG?

The grief of losing your beloved dog will be as lasting as the grief of losing a human friend or relative. In most cases, if your dog died of old age (if there is such a thing), he had slowed down considerably. Do you want a new Shih Tzu puppy to replace him? Or are you better off in finding a more mature Shih Tzu, say two to three years of age, which will be house-trained and will have an already developed personality. In this case, you can find out if you like each other after a few hours of being together.

The decision is, of course, your own. Do you want another

Many pet cemeteries have facilities for storing a dog's ashes.

Shih Tzu or perhaps a different breed so as to avoid comparison with your beloved friend? Most people usually stay with the same breed because they know (and love) the characteristics of that breed. Then, too, they often know people who have the same breed and perhaps they are lucky enough that a breeder they know and respect expects a litter soon. What could be better?

Consult your veterinarian to help you locate a pet cemetery in your area.

141

SHOWING YOUR
Shih Tzu

When you purchase your Shih Tzu, you will make it clear to the breeder whether you want one just as a lovable companion and pet, or if you hope to be buying a Shih Tzu with show prospects. No reputable breeder will sell you a young puppy and tell you that acquired is a puppy with "show potential."

To the novice, exhibiting a Shih Tzu in the show ring may look easy, but it takes a lot of hard work and devotion to do top winning at a show such as the prestigious Westminster Kennel

Few breeds are the natural show dogs that Shih Tzu are! The proud owners love to give their dogs the opportunity to show off a bit.

he is *definitely* of show quality, for so much can go wrong during the early months of a puppy's development. If you plan to show, what you will hopefully have

Club dog show, not to mention a little luck too!

The first concept that the canine novice learns when watching a dog show is that each dog first competes against members of his own breed. Once the judge has selected the best member of each breed (Best of Breed), provided that the show is judged on a Group system, that chosen dog will compete with other Best of Breed dogs in his group. Finally, the dogs chosen first in each group will compete for Best in Show.

AKC GROUPS
For showing purposes, the American Kennel Club divides its recognized breeds into seven groups: Toy Dogs, Sporting Dogs, Hounds, Working Dogs, Terriers, Non-Sporting Dogs and Herding Dogs.

The second concept that you must understand is that the dogs are not actually compared against one another. The judge compares each dog against his breed standard, the approved word depiction of the ideal specimen that is approved by the American Kennel Club (AKC). While some early breed standards were indeed based on specific dogs that were famous or popular, many dedicated enthusiasts say that a perfect specimen, as described in the standard, has never walked into a show ring, has never been bred and, to the woe of dog breeders around the globe, does not exist. Breeders attempt to get as close to this ideal as possible with every litter, but theoretically the "perfect" dog is so elusive that it is impossible. (And if the "perfect" dog were born, breeders and judges would never agree that it was indeed "perfect.")

If you are interested in exploring the world of dog showing, your best bet is to join your local breed club or the national parent club, which is the American Shih

BECOMING A CHAMPION
An official AKC champion of record requires that a dog accumulate 15 points under three different judges, including two "majors" under different judges. Points are awarded based on the number of dogs entered into competition, varying from breed to breed and place to place. A win of three, four or five points is considered a "major." The AKC annually assigns a schedule of points to adjust the variations that accompany a breed's popularity and the population of a given area.

Tzu Club, Inc. These clubs often host both regional and national specialties, shows only for Shih Tzu, which can include conformation as well as obedience and agility trials. Even if you have no intention of competing with your Shih Tzu, a specialty is like a festival for lovers of the breed who congregate to share their favorite topic: Shih

SHOW-RING ETIQUETTE

Just as with anything else, there is a certain etiquette to the show ring that can only be learned through experience. Showing your dog can be quite intimidating to you as a novice when it seems as if everyone else knows what he is doing. You can familiarize yourself with ring procedure beforehand by taking showing classes to prepare you and your dog for conformation showing and by talking with experienced handlers. When you are in the ring, it is very important to pay attention and listen to the instructions you are given by the judge about where to move your dog. Remember, even the most skilled handlers had to start somewhere. Keep it up and you too will become a proficient handler as you gain practice and experience.

Tzu! Clubs also send out newsletters, and some organize training days and seminars in order that people may learn more about their chosen breed. To locate the breed club closest to you, contact the American Kennel Club, which furnishes the rules and regulations for all of these events plus general dog registration and other basic requirements of dog ownership.

The American Kennel Club offers three kinds of conformation shows: an all-breed show (for all AKC-recognized breeds), a specialty show (for one breed only, usually sponsored by the parent club) and a Group show (for all breeds in the group).

For a dog to become an AKC champion of record, the dog must accumulate 15 points at the shows from at least three different judges, including two "majors." A "major" is defined as a three-, four- or five-point win, and the number of points per win is determined by the number of dogs entered in the show on that day. Depending on the breed, the number of points that are awarded varies. In a breed as popular as the Shih Tzu, more dogs are needed to rack up the points. At any dog show, only one dog and one bitch of each breed can win points.

Dog showing does not offer "co-ed" classes. Dogs and bitches never compete against each other

Breeders and owners take great pride in their winning dogs. This flawless show dog, one of the UK's top winners, has a handsome silver cup to sleep in tonight!

in the classes. Non-champion dogs are called "class dogs" because they compete in one of five classes. A dog is entered in a particular class depending on his age and previous show wins. To begin, there is the Puppy Class (for 6- to 9-month-olds and for 9- to 12-month-olds); this class is followed by the Novice Class (for dogs that have not won any first prizes except in the Puppy Class or three first prizes in the Novice Class and have not accumulated any points toward their champion title); the Bred-by-Exhibitor Class (for dogs handled by their breeders or handled by one of the breeder's immediate family); the American-bred Class (for dogs bred in the US); and the Open Class (for any dog that is not a champion).

FIVE CLASSES AT SHOWS

At most AKC all-breed shows, there are five regular classes offered: Puppy, Novice, Bred-by-Exhibitor, American-bred and Open. The Puppy Class is usually divided as 6 to 9 months of age and 9 to 12 months of age. When deciding in which class to enter your dog, male or female, you must carefully check the show schedule to make sure that you have selected the right class. Depending on the age of the dog, previous first-place wins and the sex of the dog, you must make the best choice. It is possible to enter a one-year-old dog who has not won sufficient first places in any of the non-Puppy Classes, though the competition is more intense the further you progress from the Puppy Class.

A sure indicator of a dog's proper construction is his gait. Only a dog that is properly put together will move with the desired gait.

The judge at the show begins judging the Puppy Class, first dogs and then bitches, and proceeds through the classes. The judge places his winners first through fourth in each class. In the Winners Class, the first-place winners of each class compete with one another to determine Winners Dog and Winners Bitch. The judge also places a Reserve Winners Dog and Reserve Winners Bitch, which could be awarded the points in the case of a disqualification. The Winners Dog and Winners Bitch, the two that are awarded the points for the breed, then compete with any champions of record entered in the show, who are called "specials." The judge reviews the Winners Dog, Winners Bitch and all the other champions to select his Best of Breed. The Best of Winners is selected between the Winners Dog and Winners Bitch. Were one of these two to be selected Best of Breed, he would automatically be named Best of Winners as well. Finally the judge selects his Best of Opposite Sex to the Best of Breed winner.

At a Group show or all-breed show, the Best of Breed winners from each breed then compete against one another for Group One through Group Four. The judge compares each Best of Breed to his breed standard, and the dog that most closely lives up to the ideal for his breed is selected as Group One. Finally, all seven group winners (from the Toy Group, Sporting Group, Hound Group, etc.) compete for Best in Show.

Your winning entry could garner a ribbon, a trophy or a medal, depending on the venue and the type of contest.

To find out about dog shows in your area, you can subscribe to the American Kennel Club's monthly magazine, the *American Kennel Gazette* and the accompanying *Events Calendar*. You can also look in your local newspaper for advertisements for dog shows in your area or go on the Internet to the AKC's website, www.akc.org.

If your Shih Tzu is six months of age or older and registered with the AKC, you can enter him in a dog show where the breed is offered classes. Provided that your Shih Tzu does not have a disqualifying fault, he can compete. Only unaltered dogs can be entered in a dog show, so if you have spayed or neutered your Shih Tzu, you cannot compete in conformation shows. The reason for this is simple. Dog shows are the main forum to prove which representatives in a breed are worthy of being bred. Only dogs that have achieved championships—the AKC "seal of approval" for quality in pure-bred dogs—should be bred. Altered dogs, however, can participate in other AKC events such as obedience trials and the Canine Good Citizen program.

HANDLING
Before you actually step into the ring, you would be well advised to sit back and observe the judge's ring procedure. If it is your first time in the ring, stand back and study how the exhibitor in front of you is performing. The judge asks each handler to "stack" the dog, hopefully showing the dog

147

The A-frame is a common obstacle in agility trials.

off to his best advantage. The judge will observe the dog from a distance and from different angles, and approach the dog to check his teeth, overall structure, alertness and muscle tone, as well as consider how well the dog "conforms" to the standard. Most importantly, the judge will have the exhibitor move the dog around the ring in some pattern

INFORMATION ON CLUBS

You can get information about dog shows from the national kennel clubs:

American Kennel Club
5580 Centerview Dr.,
Raleigh, NC 27606-3390
www.akc.org

United Kennel Club
100 E. Kilgore Road,
Kalamazoo, MI 49002
www.ukcdogs.com

Canadian Kennel Club
89 Skyway Ave., Suite 100,
Etobicoke, Ontario
M9W 6R4 Canada
www.ckc.ca

The Kennel Club
1-5 Clarges St., Piccadilly,
London W1Y 8AB, UK
www.the-kennel-club.org.uk

that he should specify (another advantage to not going first, but always listen since some judges change their directions—and the judge is always right!). Finally, the judge will give the dog one last look before moving on to the next exhibitor.

If you are not in the top four in your class at your first show, do not be discouraged. Be patient and consistent, and you may eventually find yourself in a winning line-up. Remember that the winners were once in your shoes and have devoted many hours and much money to earn the placement. If you find that your dog is losing every time and never getting a nod, it may be time to consider a different dog sport or to just enjoy your Shih Tzu as a pet. Parent clubs offer other events, such as agility, tracking, obedience, instinct tests and more, which may be of interest to the owner of a well-trained Shih Tzu.

OBEDIENCE TRIALS

Obedience trials in the US trace back to the early 1930s when organized obedience training was developed to demonstrate how well dog and owner could work together. The pioneer of obedience trials is Mrs. Helen Whitehouse Walker, a Standard Poodle fancier, who designed a series of exercises after the Associated Sheep, Police Army Dog Society of Great Britain. Since the early days, obedience trials have grown by leaps and bounds, and today there are over 2,000 trials held in the US every year, with more than 100,000 dogs competing. Any AKC-registered dog can enter an obedience trial, regardless of conformational disqualifications or neutering.

At agility trials, the Shih Tzu is motivated, agile and success-oriented! This contestant is on the seesaw.

Obedience trials are divided into three levels of progressive difficulty. At the first level, the Novice, dogs compete for the title Companion Dog (CD); at the intermediate level, the Open, dogs compete for the title Companion Dog Excellent (CDX); and at the advanced level, the Utility, dogs compete for the title Utility Dog (UD). Classes are sub-divided into "A" (for beginners) and "B" (for more experienced handlers). A perfect score at any level is 200, and a dog must score 170 or better to earn a "leg," of which three are needed to earn the title. To earn points, the dog must score more than 50% of the available points in each exercise; the possible points range from 20 to 40.

Each level consists of a different set of exercises. In the Novice level, the dog must heel on and off lead, come, long sit, long down and stand for examination. These skills are the basic ones required for a well-behaved "Companion Dog." The Open level requires that the dog perform the same exercises as above but without a leash for extended lengths of time, as well as retrieve a dumbbell, broad jump and drop on recall. In the Utility level, dogs must perform ten difficult exercises, including scent discrimination, hand signals for basic commands, directed jump and directed retrieve.

Once a dog has earned the UD title, he can compete with other proven obedience dogs for the coveted title of Utility Dog Excellent (UDX), which requires that the dog win "legs" in ten shows. Utility Dogs who earn "legs" in Open B and Utility B earn points toward their Obedience Trial Champion title. In 1977 the title Obedience Trial Champion (OTCh.) was established by the AKC. To become an OTCh., a dog needs to earn 100 points, which requires three first places in Open B and Utility under three different judges.

The Grand Prix of obedience trials, the AKC National Obedience Invitational gives qualifying Utility Dogs the chance to win the newest and highest title: National Obedience Champion (NOC). Only the top 25 ranked obedience dogs, plus any dog ranked in the top 3 in his breed, are allowed to compete.

TRACKING

Any dog is capable of tracking, using his nose to follow a trail. Tracking tests are exciting and competitive ways to test your Shih Tzu's instinctive scenting ability. The AKC started tracking tests in 1937, when the first AKC-licensed test took place as part of the Utility level at an obedience trial. Ten years later in 1947, the AKC offered the first title, Tracking Dog (TD). It was not until 1980 that the AKC added the Tracking Dog Excellent title (TDX), which was followed by the Versatile Surface Tracking title (VST) in 1995. The title Champion Tracker (CT) is awarded to a dog who has earned all three titles.

In the beginning level of tracking, the owner follows the dog

CANINE GOOD CITIZEN® PROGRAM

Have you ever considered getting your dog "certified"? The AKC's Canine Good Citizen® Program affords your dog just that opportunity. Using the basic training and good manners you have taught him, your well-behaved canine citizen takes a series of ten tests that illustrate that he can behave properly at home, in a public place and around other dogs. The tests are administered by participating dog clubs, colleges, 4-H clubs, scouts and other community groups and are open to all pure-bred and mixed-breed dogs. Upon passing the ten tests, the suffix CGC is then applied to your dog's name.

The ten tests are: 1. Accepting a friendly stranger; 2. Sitting politely for petting; 3. Appearance and grooming; 4. Walking on a lead; 5. Walking through a group of people; 6. Sit, down and stay on command; 7. Coming when called; 8. Meeting another dog; 9. Calm reaction to distractions; 10. Separation from owner.

Pipe tunnels and collapsed tunnels pose no challenge to the trained Shih Tzu.

through a field on a long lead. To earn the TD title, the dog must follow a track laid by a human 30 to 120 minutes prior. The track is about 500 yards with up to 5 directional changes. The TDX requires that the dog follow a track that is 3 to 5 hours old over a course up to 1,000 yards with up to 7 directional changes. The VST requires that the dog follow a track up to 5 hours old through an urban setting.

AGILITY TRIALS

Having had its origins in the UK back in 1977, AKC agility had its official beginning in the US in August 1994, when the first licensed agility trials were held. The AKC allows all registered breeds (including Miscellaneous Class breeds) to participate, providing the dog is 12 months of age or older. Agility is designed so that the handler demonstrates how well the dog can work at his side. The handler directs his dog over an obstacle course that includes jumps as well as tires, the dog walk, weave poles, pipe tunnels, collapsed tunnels, etc. While working his way through the course, the dog must keep one eye and ear on the handler and the rest of his body on the course. The handler gives verbal commands and hand signals to guide the dog through the course.

Agility is great fun for dog and owner, with many rewards for everyone involved. Interested owners should join a training club that has obstacles and experienced agility handlers who can introduce you and your dog to the "ropes" (and tires, tunnels, etc.).

The world's oldest dog show is the Westminster Kennel Club Dog Show, which takes place annually in New York City. The group finales are completely televised, and the show has an attendance of more than 50,000 people per day.

AMERICAN KENNEL CLUB TITLES

The AKC offers over 40 different titles to dogs in competition. Depending on the events that your dog can enter, different titles apply. Some titles can be applied as prefixes, meaning that they are placed before the dog's name (e.g., Ch. King of the Road) and others are used as suffixes, placed after the dog's name (e.g., King of the Road, CD).

These titles are used as prefixes:

Conformation Dog Shows
• Ch. (Champion)
Obedience Trials
• NOC (National Obedience Champion)
• OTCH (Obedience Trial Champion)
• VCCH (Versatile Companion Champion)
Tracking Tests
• CT [Champion Tracker (TD,TDX and VST)]
Agility Trials
• MACH (Master Agility Champion)
• MACH2, MACH3, MACH4, etc.
Field Trials
• FC (Field Champion)
• AFC (Amateur Field Champion)
• NFC (National Field Champion)
• NAFC (National Amateur Field Champion)
• NOGDC (National Open Gun Dog Champion)
• AKC GDSC (AKC Gun Dog Stake Champion)
• AKC RGDSC (AKC Retrieving Gun Dog Stake Champion)
Herding Trials
• HC (Herding Champion)
Dual
• DC (Dual Champion — Ch. and FC)
Triple
• TC (Triple Champion — Ch., FC and OTCH)
Coonhounds
• NCH (Nite Champion)
• GNCH (Grand Nite Champion)
• SHNCH (Senior Grand Nite Champion)
• GCH (Senior Champion)
• SGCH (Senior Grand Champion)
• GFC (Grand Field Champion)
• SGFC (Senior Grand Field Champion)
• WCH (Water Race Champion)
• GWCH (Water Race Grand Champion)
• SGWCH (Senior Grand Water Race Champion)

These titles are used as suffixes:

Obedience
• CD (Companion Dog)
• CDX (Companion Dog Excellent)
• UD (Utility Dog)
• UDX (Utility Dog Excellent)
• VCD1 (Versatile Companion Dog 1)
• VCD2 (Versatile Companion Dog 2)
• VCD3 (Versatile Companion Dog 3)
• VCD4 (Versatile Companion Dog 4)
Tracking Tests
• TD (Tracking Dog)
• TDX (Tracking Dog Excellent)
• VST (Variable Surface Tracker)
Agility Trials
• NA (Novice Agility)
• OA (Open Agility)
• AX (Agility Excellent)
• MX (Master Agility Excellent)
• NAJ (Novice Jumpers with weaves)
• OAJ (Open Jumpers with weaves)
• AXJ (Excellent Jumpers with weaves)
• MXJ (Master Excellent Jumpers with weaves)
Hunting Test
• JH (Junior Hunter)
• SH (Senior Hunter)
• MH (Master Hunter)
Herding Test
• HT (Herding Tested)
• PT (Pre-Trial Tested)
• HS (Herding Started)
• HI (Herding Intermediate)
• HX (Herding Excellent)
Lure Coursing
• JC (Junior Courser)
• SC (Senior Courser)
• MC (Master Courser)
Earthdog
• JE (Junior Earthdog)
• SE (Senior Earthdog)
• ME (Master Earthdog)
Lure Coursing
• JC (Junior Courser)
• SC (Senior Courser)
• MC (Master Courser)

JUNIOR SHOWMANSHIP

For budding dog handlers, ages 10 to 18 years, Junior Showmanship competitions are an excellent training ground for the next generation of dog professionals. Owning and caring for a dog are wonderful methods of teaching children responsibility, and Junior Showmanship builds upon that foundation. Juniors learn by grooming, handling and training their dogs, and the quality of junior's presentation of the dog (and himself) is evaluated by a licensed judge. The junior can enter with any registered AKC dog to compete, including an ILP, provided that the dog lives with him or a member of his family.

Junior Showmanship competitions are divided into two classes: Novice (for beginners) and Open (for juniors show have three first place wins in the Novice Class). The junior must run with the dog with the rest of the handlers and dogs, stack the dog for examination and individually gait the dog in a specific pattern. Juniors should practice with a handling class or an experienced handler before entering the Novice Class so that they recognize all the jargon that the judge may use in the ring.

A National Junior Organization was founded in 1997 to help promote the sport of dog showing among young people. The AKC also offers a Junior Scholarship for juniors who excel in the program.

Now you can understand why the words Shih Tzu in Chinese can be translated into lion's mane. This "lion" is proudly enthroned on his perch.

INDEX

Page numbers in **boldface** indicate illustrations.

Adult diets 66
Agility trial 105, 151
Allergies
—airborne 116
—food 116
AKC 42
Akoya Princess Tanya, 19
Alfred Kohen 20
America 18
American dog tick **124, 125**
American Kennel Club, The 18, 40, 143-144
—address 148
—*Gazette* 147
—standard 35
—registrations 22
—titles 154
American Shih Tzu Club 19, 143
Ancylostoma braziliense 129
Ancylostoma caninum **129**
Ancylostoma tubaeforme 129
Andy Hickok Warner 20
Apso and Lion Dog Club 16
Apsok 12
Ascaris lumbricoides **128**
Attention 95
Auto-immune skin conditions 116
Axelrod, Dr. Herbert R. 127
Back problems 30
Bailey, Colonel and Mrs. 16
Barking 26
Bathing 73
Bedding 49
Bell, Charles 16
Best in Show 142
Best of Breed 142, 146
Best of Opposite Sex 146
Best of Winners 146
Bite 33
Bjornholmes Pif 19
Boarding 81
Bones 51
Borrelia burgdorferi 125
Bowls 52
Breed standard 33, 143

Breeder 39, 40, 46, 57
Britain 15
Brown dog tick **127**
Brownrigg, General Sir Douglas 10, 14
Brownrigg, Lady 10, 14, 17
Buddha Manjusri 10
Buddhism 10
Burial 140
Canadian Kennel Club
—address 148
Canine development schedule 89
Canine Good Citizen 147, 150
Car 78
Cat 94
CDS 134
Cemetery 140
Cenier, Dr. 15
Challenge Certificates 17
Champion 17, 19, 143-144
Chewing 50, 62, 90
Cheyletiellosis mite 126
Chigger infestation 127
Chin Pi Yu Huang 28
China 9, 12
Choo-Choo 17
Chou Fang 8
Chow Chow 12, 16
Chumulari 20
Chumulari Hih-Hih 19
Chumulari Ying Ying 19-20
Classes 144, 145
Clark, Mrs. Eunice 19
Cleaning supplies 52
Coat 23, 31
Cognitive dysfunction syndrome 134
Collar 51, 95
Coleman, Ingrid 19
Color 41
Colors 23, 28
Colostrum 65
Colwell, Ingrid 19, 20
Come 100
Commands 86, 96-103
Commitment 38, 44
Companion Dog 149
Companion Dog Excellent 149

Continent 21
Control 88
Coronavirus 114, 117
Countess d'Anjou 11, 21
Crate 47-48, 63, 79, 88, 92
—training 48, 92
Crying 62
Ctenocephalides canis **120, 122**
Curtis, Mr. 19
Cushing's disease 137
Cutaneous larva migrans syndrome 129
Czech Republic 21
Dalai Lama 14
Deer tick **125**
Denmark 21
Denning instinct 49
Dental examination 114
Dental health 116
Dentition 33
Dermacentor variabilis 124-125
Dermanyssus gallinae 127
Destructive behavior 138
Dew claws 26
Deworming 115
Di Ji Anjou 11
Diabetes mellitus 137
Diet
—adults 66
—grain-based 67
—puppy 65
—seniors 66
Dirofilaria immitis **133**
Discipline 93
Distemper 114, 117
Dog flea **120**
Dog tick **125**
Dowager Empress Tzu Hsi 14
Down 97
Dragonwyck The Great Gatsby 20
Drying 73
Ear cleaning 76
Easton, Rev. and Mrs. D. Allan 19, 20
Echinococcus multilocularis 130
Edel, Margaret 20
Elizabeth I 17
Europe 21
Euthanasia 139, 140

Eutrombicula alfreddugesi 127
Events Calendar 147
Exercise 68
External parasites 120-127
Eye problems 31
Fat 119
Feet 71
Fence 55
First aid 111
Flea 120-124, 130
—life cycle 121-122
Follicular mange 126
Food 64
—allergy 116
—intolerance 117
—preference 65
—problems 118
—storage 64
—treats 103
Fowler, Audrey 19
Gait 34, 37
Geusendam, Erika 21
Great Britain 12
Grooming 68-78
Groups 142
Ha-pa 11
Hair 119
Halter 53
Handling 147
Head 22-23
Health 28, 109
—dental 116
Heart disease 30
Heartworm 114, 132-133
—life cycle **130**
—preventatives 129, 131
Heel 102
Height 22
Hepatitis 114, 117
Hereditary problems 28
—skin disorders 115
Hibou 15
Hip dysplasia 114
Home preparation 47
Home safety 54
Hookworm **129**
Housebreaking 86-93
—schedule 90

Housing 87
Hutchins, Miss E. M. 10, 15
ID tags 51, 83
Identification 82
IGR 122, 124
Insect Growth Regulator 122, 124
Insurance 43
Internal parasites 127-133
Ireland 10
Jemima of Lhakang 20
Judge 146
Jungfaltets Wu-Pa 20
Jungfeltets Jung Wu 19
Junior Showmanship 155
K'ai Fu, 12
Kennel Club, The 15-16
—address 148
Kennel cough 114, 117
Kibler, Bill and Joan 20
Koo, Mme. Wellington 15
Kublai Khan 10
Lakoya Princess Tanya Shu 20
Lead 51, 95
Lee, Madam Lu Zuen 25
Leptospirosis 114, 117
Lhasa Apso 9, 10-11, 13, 17, 18, 23
Lice 126
Life expectancy 135
Lion 10
Lung-fu-ssu 15-16
Lupus 116
Madam Ko of Taishan 17
Mange mite 126
Mar-Del's Ring-A-Ding-Ding 20
Margaret Easton 19
Mary and Jack Woods 20
Mei Mei 15
Microchip 83
Milk 65
Miscellaneous Class 18
Mites 76, 125
Mouth 33
Movement 34, 37
Mythology 9
Nail clipping 76
National Obedience Invitational
  150
Neutering 110, 112, 114

Nipping 61
Norway 21
Nose 28, 33
Obedience class 84, 104
Obedience Trial Champion 150
Obedience trials 149
Obesity 68, 138
OK 102
Old dog syndrome 134
Otodectes cynotis 127
Our Dogs 17
Ownership 44
Pai 12
Pads 71
Parainfluenza 114
Parasite
—bites 115
  external 120-127
  internal 127-133
Parvovirus 114, 117
Pat Semones Durham 20
Patton, Norman 20
Pauptit, Eta 21
Pekingese 14-15, 18, 23
Personality 26
Pet trim 73
Physical characteristics 22
Pien Ta Shiu Chiu 28
Poisonous plants 118
Preventative medicine 110, 136
Psoroptes bovis 126
Puffs 28
Pug 13-14
Punishment 94
Puppy
—appearance 41
—buying 40
—family introduction 56
—financial responsibility 52
—food 65
—health 112
—problems 59, 61, 63
—selection 40
—training 58, 85
Puppy-proofing 54
Rabies 114, 117
Rawhide 51
Red Cross 17

Red mange 126
Registration 19
Rhabditis 128
Rhipicephalus sanguineus 127
Rosenberg, Alva 19
Roundworm 115, 128
Sarcoptes mite 126
Scabies 126
School 95
Senior 136
—diets 66
—symptoms 138
Separation anxiety 62, 138
Shih Tzu Club of America 19
Shih Tzu Kou 14
Shock-dogs 14
Shu-ssa 15
Si-Klang Wu-Ling 19
Si Klang's Tashi 20
Sit 96
Skeleton 113
Skin problems 114
Sleeve dogs 13
Slovak Republic 21
Socialization 59
Spaying 110, 112
Specials 146
Spinal injury 30
Standard 33, 143
Stay 98
Strongyloides 131
Switzerland 11
Ta Chi of Taishan 17
Tail 26
Tangra v. Tschomo Lungma 20
Tapeworm 115, 130
Tattoo 83
Temperament 40
—evaluation 112
—testing 114
Texas Shih Tzu Society 19
Thorndike, Dr. Edward 94
Thorndike's Theory of Learning 94
Threadworms 131
Tibet 9
Tibetan Breeds Association 17-18
Tibetan Lion Dog 14
Tibetan Lion Dogs 17

Tibetan Spaniel 11, 18
Tick 124-125
Tinies 15
Toilet cleaners 54
Topknot 23-25, 77
Toxocara canis 128
Toys 49, 51, 61
Tracheobronchitis 114
Tracking 150
Training 39, 61
—crate 92
—equipment 95
—puppy 58
Traveling 78
Treats 57, 95
Trichuris vulpis 130
UK 17
Umbilical hernias 42
Uncinaria stenocephala 129
Underline 34
United Kennel Club
—address 148
United States 12
Utility Dog 149
Vaccinations 42, 81, 112
Veterinarian 42, 55, 109, 115, 127
Veterinary specialist 110, 115
Viruses 113
Walker, Mrs. Helen Whitehouse
  149
Water 68, 88
Wei-Honey Gold of Elfann 20
Weight 22, 34
Westminster Kennel Club Dog
  Show 153
Whining 62
Whipworms 130
Winners Bitch 146
Winners Class 146
Winners Dog 146
World War II 17
Worm Control 114
Worming 42, 112
Yi Ting Mo 28

157

My Shih Tzu

PUT YOUR PUPPY'S FIRST PICTURE HERE

Dog's Name _____

Date _____ Photographer _____